Computin...
Made Simple

Access 2000 Business E...
STEPHEN
075064611X   1999

ASP   NEW!
DEANE
075065869X   2003

Basic Computer Skills
SHERMAN
075064897X   2001

CompuServe 2000
BRINDLEY
0750645245   2000

Designing Internet Hom...
2ed
HOBBS
0750644761   1999

Dreamweaver
MURPHY
0750654597   2002

ECDL/ICDL 3.0 Office 20...
Revised Edition
BCD Ltd
0750653388   2003

ECDL/ICDL 3.0 Office 97...
BCD Ltd
0750651873   2000

Excel 2002
MORRIS
0750656913   2002

Excel 2000
MORRIS
0750641800   2000

Excel 2000 Business Ed...
MORRIS
0750646098   2000

Excel 97 for Windows
MORRIS
0750638028   1997

Excel for Windows 95 (V. 7)
MORRIS
0750628162   1996

Explorer 5
MCBRIDE, P K
0750646276   1999

MURPHY
0750651903   2001

MADE SIMPLE
BOOKS

XML

Made Simple

XML
Made Simple

Sharon Deane and Robert Henderson

MADE SIMPLE
BOOKS

AMSTERDAM • BOSTON • HEIDELBERG • LONDON • NEW YORK • OXFORD
PARIS • SAN DIEGO • SAN FRANCISCO • SINGAPORE • SYDNEY • TOKYO

Made Simple
An imprint of Elsevier
Linacre House, Jordan Hill, Oxford OX2 8DP
200 Wheeler Road, Burlington, MA 01803

First published 2004

TRADEMARKS/REGISTERED TRADEMARKS
Computer hardware and software brand names mentioned in this book
are protected by their respective trademarks and are acknowledged.

British Library Cataloguing in Publication Data
A catalogue record for this book is available from the British Library

ISBN 0 7506 5998 X

For information on all Made Simple publications
visit our website at www.madesimple.co.uk

Typeset by Elle and P.K. McBride, Southampton

Icons designed by Sarah Ward © 1994
Printed and bound in Great Britain

Contents

Preface

The speed of the Internet revolution has created constant innovation but left a trail of technologies that have disappeared from view or radically changed form before being accepted. People familiar with this panoply of shifting software standards may be wondering if a similar fate will befall XML. The eXtensible Markup Language has gone through many changes over its short life and browser programs still do not offer full support for all the XML features. However, the odds on XML surviving and even becoming the core technology of the Internet are very promising.

XML at its heart is a straightforward idea – have a language for describing data and make it easy enough to change this data into a form suitable for different sorts of computing device. Precisely because of this simplicity and free availability it is likely to become the lingua franca of electronic information exchange. You now see XML being used to build documents on the World Wide Web, but it is also being utilised in databases, office programs, electronic news, publishing and multimedia.

In this book we are going to look at the history of XML and explain why it is so useful to gain a grounding in XML theory. We will show you how to create your own XML documents and the definitions which enable a computer to understand them. With the addition of style sheets, these documents will look indistinguishable from conventional web pages. We are not going to cover using programming languages such as C++ or PERL with XML as this is a topic worthy of a much larger volume. For the same reason we stick to client-side XML. This book does not cover server-side XML coding in any real detail. In later chapters we will have a little fun in using XML technologies to produce multimedia presentations and web pages viewable via a mobile phone.

If you have a web development background, XML is an essential learning requirement, but even if your skills are in another field like database administration it is worth understanding XML as it becomes more wide-spread in the computer industry.

XML is still a new and evolving technology, and certain features are not supported as widely as they ought to be. As a prerequisite, we assume that you have knowledge of HTML coding and understand the basics of web design but will include some refresher material as we go along.

All of the software packages we employ in the following chapters are either free, or available in time-limited demo packages. The two essential applications needed are a text editor you are comfortable with and the latest version of a current web browser, such as Internet Explorer 6, Mozilla or Safari. You should be able to use the programs in this book on Windows, Macintosh or Linux platforms and where appropriate we will list software for those operating systems.

Sharon Deane

Robert Henderson

1 What is XML?

Background to XML

Computer networks have existed for decades, but their usage was limited to business, academia and the military because the technologies were far too expensive for average consumers. When processing power began to explode in the late 1970s, smaller 'personal' computers became cheap enough to be household items and an essential tool for every business.

When computers are used to swap documents, the data enclosed within them must be encoded in an efficient way. The most popular encoding method is *ASCII* – the American Standard Code for Information Interchange. ASCII code is built around the byte – an 8 bit storage unit – with 7 bits used and the eighth tending to be free or used for error-correcting. With 7 bits you can hold 128 values. This is enough for all the letters of the English language, both in upper and lower case, punctuation marks and numbers. In ASCII the first 31 codes are used to denote control codes such as start/end of transmission, new line and so on. A space is 32, and the alphabet starts with the capital letters at 65, so 65 = A, 66 = B, etc.

The message HI THERE is encoded as:

72,73,32,84,72,69,82,69

Markup

The ASCII system works well for unformatted text files (such as computer programs), but is not adequate for transmitting documents with typographical information. To display a newspaper or magazine article you need to know how the text is spaced, the size of the letters, the look of the lettering (font), whether it is in rows or columns and so on. To solve this problem *markup* languages were created – making electronic, the typesetter's hand-written ('marked-up') instructions.

When describing formatting we still have our text to be displayed, but extra codes are added to it, that do not represent displayed characters. These are still in the traditional ASCII format, but the computer knows to process them differently. For instance, in early word processors, the user would have a variety of 'control codes' for representing how text should look – an extension of the already existing coding system in ASCII. In a markup language entire words would represent instructions to the computer. To differentiate between these and data, the instructions would be enclosed between brackets. Such words are called *tags*. Some tags have attributes – extra values passed to them. For example a tag to describe a font will perhaps have an attribute describing the font type, and one specifying size.

SGML

Describing documents is surprisingly complicated – different users require their own special functions and so a variety of electronic markup systems have appeared since the 1960s – most of them wholly incompatible with each other.

In the late 1960s Charles Goldfarb and his team of IBM researchers were studying electronic document systems and created a comprehensive language that described text formatting and markup. This was known as *GML* (Generalized Markup Language – and also the initials of its creators, Goldfarb, Mosher and Lorie). Because of IBM's market stature, GML was widely used and seen as a good base for building a more standard document description language.

The first working draft of the new Standard Generalized Markup Language (SGML) was released in 1980, and finally accepted by the ISO in 1986.

SGML is a *metalanguage*, that is, a language which is used to describe the structure of another language. Hence SGML isn't actually a document language itself but should be seen as a platform-independent basis for building adapted markup languages based on a common structure. All of the markup languages that we use today are in essence subsets of SGML. As a system, SGML is powerful as it allows for the creation and implementation of small tailored markup applications used for anything you can imagine.

This seems to be a little like solving a problem by making it worse – if there are a number of incompatible document languages, what is the point of creating a standard that allows even more people to invent their own?

The answer is that SGML is structured so the underlying grammar of all SGML languages should be the same, what changes is the meaning of the individual tags. What makes SGML significant is that it allows the development of something

Take note

The International Organization for Standardization (ISO) is a non-governmental body that coordinates standards for products of all types. It is comprised of members from business, academia and governments from around the world, and seeks to create standards that are recognised internationally. For more information, see their website: http://www.iso.ch

called *Document Type Definitions (DTDs)*, which are applied to describe the way in which markup expresses the content and structure of a text document.

When engineers create a new language with SGML they provide a DTD that explains what each tag should do. A computer that supports SGML can therefore distinguish any new SGML subset as long as it has a correct DTD to refer to.

This is very similar to what humans do – if your first language is German you will have a detailed knowledge of German grammar (the SGML rules). Now, if you are given a difficult technical document to understand in that language, you will know it is German just by looking at it. With an appropriate lexicon (the DTD) listing the unfamiliar words and their meanings you can eventually make sense of the document, no matter how complicated it may be.

Furthermore, because SGML rules are so general and are geared to describing data and structure, it does not matter where the documents are viewed. An SGML document may refer to data that will be printed out, viewed on a screen, or sent between machines and never actually viewed by a human. Hence SGML can be used in a wide variety of industries.

The downside with this power is that SGML was never meant to be used on small computers. It is a massive specification built up over a decade and has features irrelevant to the vast majority of users. As such, there was little point in trying to implement the SGML standard inside a typical PC. The first widespread use of basic SGML concepts came with the arrival of the World Wide Web, and its language – HTML.

The Web and HTML

In 1945 one of America's top scientists Vannevar Bush wrote an essay entitled 'As We May Think'. In this short document he set forward his ideas on a future world information retrieval system called the 'Memex'. Bush theorised that such a system would allow a person, from the comfort of their desk, to access the world's libraries electronically, and jump from document to document with ease. Bush was one of the early pioneers of electronic computers and understood what might be possible in the future, but to the average reader the idea of a small electronic retrieval system used by the individual was strictly in the realms of science fiction.

Over the years the concepts expressed in *As We May Think* came to influence a new generation of technologists, two of whom, Douglas Englebart and Ted Nelson, helped to forge the kinds of computer systems we now use (and are similar to Bush's vision). Englebart worked on information retrieval systems and among other things invented the first computer mouse and windows system (known as a graphical user interface or GUI) which he premiered in 1968. Nelson was a strong advocate of personal computing and of an easy user interface. He coined the term 'hypertext'. A hypertext system is one where (as with the Memex) documents are massively linked together and the user can navigate easily through them.

For a viable hypertext system the computer needs facilities similar to Englebart's demonstration machine, but such technology didn't become affordable to a mass audience until the mid-1980s. The Apple Macintosh had a GUI and users could control the computer by clicking with their mouse. Other machines like the Atari ST and Amiga opted for the same kind of usability. Eventually the mainstream PC market (based around the Microsoft/Intel/IBM standard) adopted similar technologies and computers with mice and graphical user interfaces became the norm.

In 1989 a researcher working for the European particle physics research organisation CERN created a straightforward hypertext system for keeping track of electronic documents. Tim Berners-Lee's first system Enquire soon evolved into the prototype for what we now call the World Wide Web, and used a SGML subset, *HTML* (HyperText Markup Language). The Web has become the part of the Internet most people are familiar with. Electronic documents are viewed with a browser program, and each document has a collection of hyperlinks which connect to other pages. Pages can be located anywhere on the planet – their location is described by a web page address – the *URL* (Uniform Resource Locator).

HTML described

An HTML document consists of a header in which information about the page such as the title is defined, and a body component that holds the page content. Generally a piece of data is surrounded by an opening and closing tag, and its function is applied to whatever is between them. The entire page begins with a **<html>** opening tag and ends with a **</html>** closing tag (note the slash), which tell the computer that the code enclosed by them is compatible with a standard web browser.

This line of code instructs the browser to display the text in header size 1 (large):

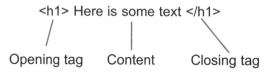

HTML became instantly popular with the academic community and soon several web-browsing applications were available (such as Mosaic). The web took off rapidly with the release of Netscape's browser, and other companies soon entered the market. Additions were made to HTML, but there was not a central authority devoted to web standards. As the web industry was changing at an accelerating rate there was a real danger that web standards could be controlled by a minority of big market players.

This situation changed with the formation of the World Wide Web Consortium (abbreviated to W3C), founded by Berners-Lee in 1994. In a similar role to the ISO the W3C has developed a series of specifications for Internet technologies with a view to making an efficient web, available to all persons who wish to use it.

Tip

The World Wide Web Consortium is the most important place for learning about upcoming Internet technologies. Their site contains downloadable specifications for over 50 Internet and web-related systems. You can find the W3C at: www.w3.org

Go to the New Visitors link and browse through some of the tutorials and information for the general reader, before looking at the (often highly technical) specification documents. The XML technologies we will look at, all have detailed references there.

HTML shortcomings

HTML has gone through multiple upgrades over the years and together with its associated technologies (style sheets, scripting languages, plug-in components) can display even the most complicated media-rich web sites. Even with this power HTML is seen as too limited for the rapidly evolving Internet.

There are several reasons for this. First, HTML is mainly geared towards appearance – HTML tags describe how the content should look – not what it is for. This distinction seems slightly pedantic – after all, if we can make a web page look like anything we want, why should we worry about ascribing meaning to the data within it? However, we do need our web documents to be amenable to search engine systems. Businesses are putting many of their important documents online and a large company might have a web site containing hundreds of thousands of pages of information. These pages all look the same to the servers they're based on – strings of tags describing font height, colour, table dimensions and so on. Finding useful information can be almost impossible.

Think about how a typical search engine works – searching technology has advanced considerably and 'hits' are calculated using a stream of complicated statistical processing based around the number of sites that link to yours as well as its estimated popularity. It is apparent that even the best search sites tend to be 'dumb' and throw up a mass of irrelevant information for many queries. Calling-up and displaying all this useless data consumes valuable computing resources.

We require a way of attaching meaning –metadata – to parts of individual documents, so the computer can process them more efficiently. The only way to do this with HTML is by using the **<meta>** tag. This has several functions, one of which allows a developer to place a list of keywords in the header of a document to facilitate easier searching. In theory, a well-used meta tag should reduce issues with searching but the system is too open to abuse. Unscrupulous programmers will put dozens (or even hundreds) of irrelevant words in a page description in the hope that search engines will pull their particular site ahead of other similar ones. The situation is so bad that many search engines either don't use the data from meta tags or treat it as a minor contributing factor to the overall search result.

Another weakness of HTML is that it comes from an era when the majority of users accessed data through a typical PC connected to a phone line. In recent years smaller computing devices have become more widely available and it is expected that soon more people will access information networks via their mobile phones

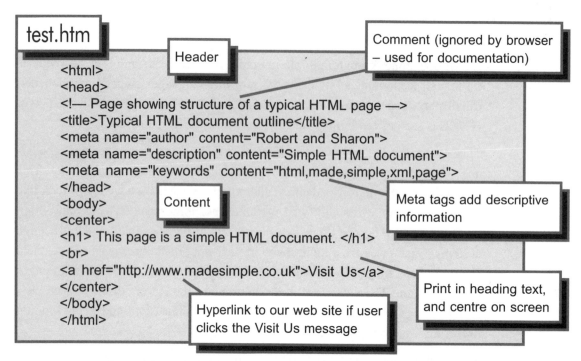

```
test.htm

                    Header                    Comment (ignored by browser
<html>                                        – used for documentation)
<head>
<!— Page showing structure of a typical HTML page —>
<title>Typical HTML document outline</title>
<meta name="author" content="Robert and Sharon">
<meta name="description" content="Simple HTML document">
<meta name="keywords" content="html,made,simple,xml,page">
</head>
<body>       Content                           Meta tags add descriptive
<center>                                      information
<h1> This page is a simple HTML document. </h1>
<br>
<a href="http://www.madesimple.co.uk">Visit Us</a>
</center>                                      Print in heading text,
</body>        Hyperlink to our web site if user   and centre on screen
</html>        clicks the Visit Us message
```

than with traditional PCs. Getting a web document to display the same on all the major browser applications can be tricky enough, adapting them to fit on tiny, often monochrome phone screens is a near impossibility.

Many of the cross-browser problems are due to the way HTML is implemented in different programs. Companies have not rigidly stuck to the HTML specification and some have added their own non-standard tags to the language. Furthermore, HTML was not designed to be a strict language – it was there to enable easy document access, not make programmers stick to software engineering conventions. You can fill an HTML page full of mistakes, or miss out important tags and it will still work on a percentage of machines. The browser will not tell you about any bugs but will either ignore them or attempt to display the incorrect content.

Dealing with incomplete code takes up extra computing resources and does nothing to discourage the problem in future. Any new Internet language must deal with these issues appropriately.

What is needed is a language that defines the data generally, and then a program (or set of program standards) tailoring content to different platforms. A simplified version of SGML combined with presentation capabilities would be ideal.

XML is the best attempt so far at fulfilling all these requirements.

The Extensible Markup Language

SGML is comprehensive and powerful, while HTML is simple to implement and a standard recognised by over 100 million web users. But each has major disadvantages – SGML's complexity is not needed for typical applications, while HTML's lack of data description renders it impotent for data processing. To overcome these problems, the W3C set to work on creating a new standard for markup languages on the Internet, based on a simplified version of SGML. The initial XML concepts emerged in 1996, and by 1998 XML version 1.0 became an official W3C standard. XML itself describes the structure of data (like SGML), but there are a related series of technologies that define how documents should look (XSL) and even how they should hyperlink to each other (XLink).

An XML document looks very similar to HTML – the distinction being that the first line will have the XML identifier and some of the tags will have different names.

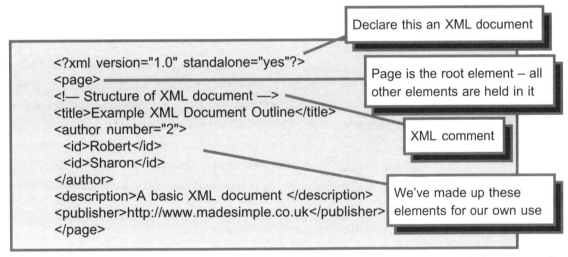

```
<?xml version="1.0" standalone="yes"?>
<page>
<!— Structure of XML document —>
<title>Example XML Document Outline</title>
<author number="2">
  <id>Robert</id>
  <id>Sharon</id>
</author>
<description>A basic XML document </description>
<publisher>http://www.madesimple.co.uk</publisher>
</page>
```

Declare this an XML document

Page is the root element – all other elements are held in it

XML comment

We've made up these elements for our own use

This is the core advantage of XML; like SGML, users can create their own tags for different uses. If a Document Type Definition is referenced with the XML, any XML-compatible software should be able to make sense of it.

Type the above listing into a text editor and save it, then open it in your browser.

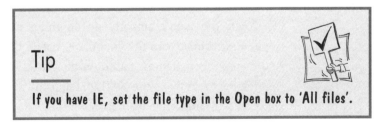

Tip

If you have IE, set the file type in the Open box to 'All files'.

You won't see a great deal. If you run Internet Explorer you'll be presented with a formatted version of the code, with different tags highlighted in different colours If you run a browser like Opera you'll only see the data held within the elements.

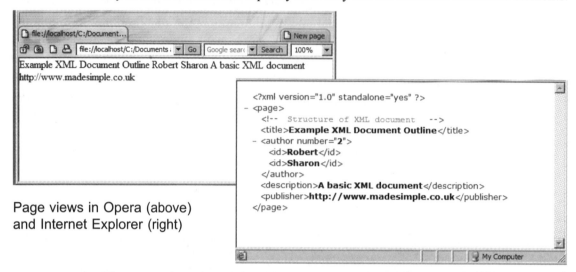

Page views in Opera (above) and Internet Explorer (right)

The structuring of XML is strict – if you make a mistake, the computer will let you know. All XML documents must be 'well-formed', that is their elements have to stick to the XML syntax rules. With an HTML page, missing tags will still result in a page displaying. Miss a single tag out in XML – or make a small blunder – and all you'll get is an error message. We deliberately added an extra slash to the closing root tag, and as you can see below the computer picked it up and marked the faulty line.

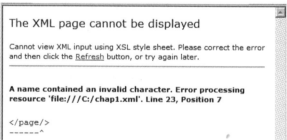

An XML file won't actually do anything unless it is loaded into a suitable application which scan the document, check that its syntax is correct ('parsing') and then perform actions based on the XML content. You do not need a special application to do this – the XML parsing software needed for the programs in this book, is built into your web browser.

Uses of XML

XML is not used simply as an interesting new way of handling web pages. Its general format allows XML documents to be used to almost any purpose. A school might have student information stored in XML files on a database. The records are easily converted to other formats automatically, so the same piece of data could be printed out, sent to another database, transformed to display on a web page for students to read or even spoken aloud with a voice-XML program. This ease of document conversion is driving the uptake of XML software. For that matter, the XML documents can be read by any technically-aware human thus making XML different to many of the data storage systems in the past that held information in an encoded format.

Consider another situation – file formats on your PC. When you type up a piece of writing on your word processor, the format that data is stored in is specific to the package you used. Some packages can load data in many formats but usually with some loss of formatting (you can save practically any document as plain text but that will lose all formatting). In the future can you even be sure there will be conversion programs to read all your old files? In theory, XML can solve this problem and some companies already have functions for saving files in XML format. Though commercial considerations are holding back widespread adoption of XML as the all-purpose file format, more and more packages are using it.

As we have showed in the past few pages, learning how to make your own XML documents is likely to be a skill in demand for many years. The rest of this book shows you how.

Exercises

1   Decode the following short ASCII message:

83,73,77,80,76,69,32,88,77,76

2   The X in XML stands for eXtensible. What does the word mean in this context?

3   What is the main difference between the central functions of XML and HTML?

4   XML is machine-readable and can be understood by humans. Generally this is a good thing. Describe circumstances where it is a disadvantage.

Take note

The answers to these exercises can be found in the Appendices, on page 157.

2 XML documents

XML is strict

In this chapter we are going to introduce you to the rules of XML. While the idea of writing code in a strict language with no room for error sounds intimidating, this is pretty much the norm with most computer languages. Forcing the programmer to stick to a strongly structured environment actually has advantages – it encourages a more logical approach to writing code and makes sure that by the time a piece of code is running the errors that still exist are minor.

An XML system consists of several components. We start off with the *documents* – these are pages of XML code like those that you met in Chapter 1. The documents hold the instructions telling the application software what to do.

Next we have a *Document Type Definition* (DTD) that explains the structure of the XML documents. The DTD is similarly written using a text editor and can either be internal (appended to a document) or external (called by one or more documents). There may be files that give further instructions on how to display or use the XML, for instance a style sheet. You may also use an *XML schema* to describe your data in place of a DTD. The schema language is actually written in XML, with the intention of making document definitions more efficient.

After we have the XML code written, we need to pass it to an application. The application can be thought of as a two-part software system. The first part must be the XML *parser* – this scans the documents and determines if they are correct and obey the rules set out in the DTD. The second part of the application is the end process – where something is actually done with the XML code.

Let us look at an example – a typical web browser. At the outset you have a DTD describing a set of markup tags for your XML, and a collection of XML tags filled with data. A style sheet file describes the various fonts and colours the end result should be displayed in.

This information is to be shown on your web browser. If you're running a modern browser it will have at least some basic support for XML. The browser is therefore your application. When the XML is loaded, the built-in parser scans each tag and checks it doesn't violate any grammatical rules. Next, the display engine of the browser will take the code, check the stylesheet and apply the style instructions to the XML, producing the final output.

What makes a document?

What rules do we have to follow in order to build XML documents? In reality, there are not many and they are quite logical. An XML document must be *well-formed*, and *valid*. Validity means the document has a DTD or schema and obeys the rules set down in it. Well-formed means that the document follows the correct XML structure.

Our first rule is that an XML document must identify itself with a *declaration*. This consists of an identifier for XML and sometimes other attributes for the character set used (the *encoding* attribute) and whether the document is loaded on its own or with other documents (*standalone* attribute). With few exceptions (a possible one being the way some multimedia browsers do not require the declaration when using the SMIL language – see Chapter 8), all documents must state in their first line that they actually are XML-based. The declaration line opens with a bracket and a question mark, and closes with a question mark and a bracket:

```
<?xml version="1.0" encoding="UTF-8" standalone="no"?>
```

Next we have lines that describe any external documents used. Here we would therefore reference the DTD and (if we are using one) the stylesheet. The example below has a declaration and link to a cascading stylesheet (see Chapter 4):

```
<?xml-stylesheet  href="style.css" type="text/css"?>
```

Trees and roots

Computer scientists have spent many years working out efficient ways of representing data. One of the most useful data structures is called a *tree*. In a tree structure data starts off with a *root* element, and separate items (*nodes*) branch off from it. These branches can have their own branches and continue on indefinitely. XML uses a form of tree structure to organise elements. All documents have a root element. Everything must go inside the root or an error results. Elements inside the

---

Tip

In your XML documents try not to nest elements too deeply within one another. One or two levels of nesting should be sufficient. More would slow down the parser, especially if the documents are large.

---

root may themselves have other elements inside them. In computer terminology we say that a *parent* element has one or more *child* elements. Elements must be nested correctly inside one another – if you transpose two elements an error will result.

For example, we have a small XML file containing the following line, showing two nested elements. The parent element, text and a child element, bold:

    <text><bold> This is the Text </bold></text>

The bold tags are enclosed within the text tags. If we swap the two closing tags:

    <text><bold> This is the Text </text></bold>

The XML parser (running inside the browser) gives the error:

    End tag 'text' does not match the start tag 'bold'.

This kind of a common slip-up rarely results in obvious problems with HTML pages and so is likely to be made quite often by the XML beginner who learned about data languages writing pages with HTML.

If you look back at the picture on page 10 showing the XML source in Internet Explorer, you can demonstrate the tree structure. Clicking on the minus signs will collapse child elements into their parent (**<author>** is a parent element, **<id>** the child), clicking on the minus sign next to the root element **<page>** collapses the entire document so only the declaration and root elements remain visible. All branches extend from the root.

Take note
───────────
We define an element in XML as anything with opening and closing tags and the data contained within them.

Comments and spacing

You may include comments in your XML code. The computer ignores what you write inside the comment line – they are there purely to be read by other humans. We saw comments in Chapter 1. In XML they are identical to their HTML equivalents:

```
<!- Here is the comment ->
```

If you have ever hand-coded a HTML page, you will be aware that HTML truncates all spacing down to a single character. Hence in HTML text such as:

```
Computer programming
```

and

```
Computer                    programming
```

should look exactly the same on the browser. XML tends to preserve the spacing without change (there are certain exceptions, for reasons of space-saving the XML-based language for mobile phones, WML, cuts out extraneous spaces). If you load the following code snippet into your browser you will note that the browser actually strips off the spacing when it displays the code. This is done by the internal style sheets the browser uses to display XML source – the whitespace is actually still there. Click on the 'view source' file option and you will see this is the case.

```
<?xml version="1.0"?>
<page>
<space> This is my code </space>
<space> This is    my code </space>
<space>      This is my    code </space>
</page>
```

Tip

You should get into the habit of commenting code during the design stage. It makes it easier to update and maintain the code in the future.

Element rules

When you write code in HTML, you will notice that it treats upper or lower case letters as the same. In most European languages, converting between the two cases is very simple, but other languages have different rules and different character sets. XML is designed to work all over the world, and so the engineers behind it have specified that parsers treat upper and lower case letters differently. Hence the tags **\<bold\> \<BOLD\> \<Bold\> \<BolD\>** all work the same in a HTML file, but would be treated as four separate tags in XML. The convention in XML is to write nearly all your tags in lower-case.

HTML has tags that exist on their own (**\<br\>** for line break, **\<hr\>** for horizontal rule). Such tags would be invalid in XML. You must include a closing tag (even if the element holds no data – i.e. is an empty element), or failing that, add a forward slash to the end of a single tag which denotes it has both opened and closed:

    \<br\>\</br\>

or more commonly:

    \<br/\>

An element's name can be anything, but must not include spaces or begin with a number. Any that do will initiate an invalid character error by the parser. Computer languages have rules on valid characters to make reading the data easier and faster.

The following variations on the name **\<element\>** are all valid (we have omitted the closing tag for clarity):

    \<element\>   Plain text

    \<_element\> Begins with an underscore

    \<ele-ment\> Hyphenated

    \<element1\> Contains a number at the end

And these are not:

    \< element\> Begins with a space

    \<ele ment\> Contains a space

    \<7element\> Begins with a number

    \<-element\> Begins with a hyphen

Attribute rules

In XML all attribute data must be enclosed in quotation marks. Again, this makes it easy to process documents as it tells the parser exactly where the attribute values start and end. Both single and double quotation marks are valid, although the majority of programmers tend to use double quotes in their XML documents.

These tags are okay:

```
<names girls="Kirsty, Jan"/>    Attribute values enclosed in double quotes
<names girls='Kirsty, Jan'/>    Values enclosed in single quotes
```

But we'll get errors from these:

```
<names girls=Kirsty, Jan/>      No quotes around data
<names girls="Kirsty, Jan/>     Missing end quote
<names girls="Kirsty, Jan'/>    Mixed single and double quotes
```

Another way of storing attributes is to place your data is separate tags, thus converting them to child elements. The data for our girls' names is equally valid if represented via the following sequence:

```
<names>
    <girls>Kirsty</girls>
    <girls>Jan</girls>
</names>
```

Tip

Many word-processors automatically convert the first letter in a line to uppercase as they assume it marks the beginning of a sentence. This is one reason why it is best to use a text editor to write computer code.

Character encoding

In ASCII, the characters of English and some European languages can be represented by an 8-bit code. Using XML to mark up text, gives us an infinite variety of possible tags to use, so long as they are defined in a DTD or the schema language. Does this mean we can represent characters in other languages using XML tags? Theoretically yes, but a better solution would be to expand the space used to store character data wide enough to hold those of other alphabets.

If you have ever browsed on news sites, you will notice that it is common now to have sites in Japanese, Urdu, Arabic and a host of other languages. To do this, programmers use Unicode – a character system that uses two bytes (16 bits) to hold letter codes. This gives us 256 times as many characters (8 bits have 256 combinations – a 16-bit code has 256 x 256 combinations)! Hence Unicode can store up to 65,535 values – easily enough for the Korean, Russian, Arabic, Thai, Hebrew, Hindi alphabets – as well as many others.

XML documents tend to be held in Unicode format – as befits a language that will become a world-wide standard for documents. When working with XML documents, you can either save them in Unicode format, or add a message to the XML header explaining which language format you wish to use. You are unlikely to have any problems if you stick to plain English in your XML files, but the moment you start using characters in another language (or if your files are to be loaded into computers in another country), then you must declare a language type. The language type is held within the encoding attribute on your XML declaration:

```
<?xml version="1.0" encoding="UTF-8"?>
```

You will have to tell the computer what subset of Unicode you intend to store text in. Of the possible encoding parameters, you are most likely to use either UTF-8 (Universal Text Format) or ISO-8859-1 (which covers most European languages). Using one of these as your encoding format will allow the XML to hold the values of most of the characters you are likely to come across.

Tip

You can find full information about the Unicode standard on the Unicode consortium Home Page, based at: http://www.unicode.org/

Entities

An entity is a character string that actually represents other characters. This sounds slightly strange, but does make logical sense. In a typical XML document there will be some characters we cannot use as element data, because they will confuse the parser. For instance in many programming languages the same angle brackets XML uses for tags are used as comparison operators. Placing a line of computer code in an XML element might well result in an error:

```
<source> if z<>10 then z=10;  </source>
```

When readiing this line, the parser would assume the bracket after 'z' was the closing tag for **<source>** and stop processing the page.

To get around problems such as this, XML has several inbuilt codes to represent illegal characters (a more comprehensive system exists in HTML with codes such as ** ** denoting a space).

An entity starts with an ampersand, followed by the entity name or code, then a semicolon to close. Five entities are included as standard in XML, they are:

```
&gt;      > greater than symbol
&lt;      < less than  symbol
&apos;  ' apostrophe
&quot;  " double quote
&amp;   & ampersand
```

The ampersand is included as that is a special character in XML.

You can use an entity to print any available character, by writing an ampersand in front of the character's code and a semicolon after it:

```
&#code;
```

The code can either be in base 10 or hexadecimal. A hex number is denoted by placing a lower-case x in front of it. Both these references represent the letter A (which if you remember has a value of 65 in ASCII).

```
&#0065; Decimal (Base 10)
&#x0041;   Hexadecimal (Base 16)
```

This line of code features two special French characters, the à with a grave accent and the ç with a cedilla:

```
<donotlike> Je n'aime pas &#0231;&#0224;! </donotlike>
```

This will correctly be displayed as:

Je n'aime pas çà!

Tip

You can find the numerical values for characters online using the Unicode code charts: http://www.unicode.org/charts/

If you run Windows, the Character Map utility can perform the same task, giving you values in both decimal and hex.

Unparsed data

Imagine you have an XML page which you intend to show on a web browser. This page contains a large chunk of C code. Typically programs written in C have complex lines with combinations of punctuation marks and text. Ideally you want the parser to recognise that this is data, but skip over it. In theory you could replace all the offending characters with entities, but what if the source file is hundreds of lines long? Even if you do include entities, the computer will waste time processing the code fragments.

For this reason XML includes a special data type – CDATA (C for Character). Anything you place inside a CDATA block is ignored by the parser (unlike a comment, the parser recognises the CDATA will ultimately have a purpose, but that purpose will likely be inside another program).

To use CDATA in your pages use the following format:

```
<![CDATA[
stuffgoeshere
]]>
```

Example:

```
<![CDATA[
put whatever you want here, some C code perhaps:
#include <stdio.h>
main()
{
        printf("Here is some C code\nWhich is for later.\n");
}
]]>
```

Note the CDATA element is in upper-case, and also the use of square brackets – there are opening brackets before and after the CDATA keyword and two closing brackets at the end of the block. You can have as many CDATA blocks in your code as you want, but you must not attempt to nest them.

This chapter has guided you through the rules and regulations of making an XML page. The next thing we need to do is figure out how we can add logical consistency to our tags, through the use of a DTD.

Exercises

1   An XML document must be well-formed. Briefly explain what criteria the computer uses to determine this.

2   The ampersand is a special character in XML, denoted by **&** What would happen if you tried to include a plain ampersand in your code, with a line like:

```
<greeting> To Jimmy & Suzie </greeting>
```

3   There are errors in this code. How many can you spot?

```
<?xml version="1.0"? encoding="UTF">
<code>
<title><bold> My Programming Page </title></bold>
<lang favourite="list>
<prog> C & C++ </prog>
<prog> PERL    </prog>
<prog> Java <prog/>
</lang>
<code>
</xml>
```

3 Document Type Definition

DTDs and XML documents

A well-formed XML document will have an XML declaration, root element, child elements that are nested correctly and so on. It can happily exist on its own, but for extra logical consistency, we will need a *Document Type Definition*. A DTD describes every element in a document and explains how they relate to one another. It is an additional layer of grammar. If XML code uses a DTD and is consistent with the DTD grammar, then we say the document is *valid*. As we saw earlier, the two prerequisites for excellent XML code are that it is well-formed and validated.

XML-based languages have their own DTD that defines how their tags and attributes interact in the overall tree structure that makes up their code. While you may always use externals DTDs, knowing how to build your own comes in very useful. When you create a DTD you are giving instructions that all documents which use it must follow the same rules. Imagine you work in a company and are asked to use XML to store customer records. Ultimately there may be thousands of XML documents on the system. If record files use your DTD, and someone tries to enter into a form an element name or property other than those that you have specified, the document will be flagged as non-valid and the originator forced to change it. A further advantage is that you can declare entities to replace chunks of text. Any text that repeatedly occurs (e.g. a name or address) can be stored as an entity, making the job of creating new documents faster and more efficient.

Your DTD may be internal to one document or an external file referenced by many users at the same time. To tell the parser that your document needs to call a DTD, the element **DOCTYPE** is used, placed just after the XML declaration. DOCTYPE can either contain the actual DTD code itself, or an URL to the external DTD.

A typical DOCTYPE line looks like this:

```
<!DOCTYPE code SYSTEM "code.dtd">
```

The word 'code' is actually the name of a root element in the XML page the DTD refers to. The second occurrence of 'code' refers to the filename of the DTD. In this case the file is on the local machine so we prefix the location with the word **SYSTEM**. If we wish the DTD to be available to other people, we add the term **PUBLIC** instead. Instead of having a plain filename, a URL can be included:

```
<!DOCTYPE code SYSTEM "http://www.outonthenet.com/code.dtd">
```

Locating a resource on the Internet can be fraught with dangers – what if a site containing your file is not available? What if the file is moved? To help remedy these possible dilemmas, the DOCTYPE can contain another system for locating a DTD. The *Formal Public Identifier* (FPI) consists of four fields of data separated by twin forward slashes. The FPI fields are:

- Field 1: Is the DTD an official standard, like HTML 4.0 for instance? If so then place a plus sign at the start of your FPI. If the DTD is one you have made yourself, or was created by a software company but not an official standard, add a minus sign.

- Field 2: You write the name of the software team responsible for the DTD here.

- Field 3: Contains the document name and version number. In the case of a document type definition file, place the word 'DTD' followed by a space and the name.

- Field 4: A two-letter code representing the language used in the document (EN for English, RU for Russian, ES for Spanish, FR for French, together with around 100 codes for the world's major languages).

Here is the document type declaration for HTML 4.0:

```
<!DOCTYPE HTML PUBLIC "-//W3C//DTD HTML 4.01//EN"
          "http://www.w3.org/TR/html4/strict.dtd">
```

After the **DOCTYPE** we see the word **HTML**. As we know, this corresponds to the root element of the HTML language (documents should begin with **<html>** and end with **</html>**) – the word **PUBLIC** is included too because this document is meant to be seen by anybody. Next comes our FPI, starting with a minus sign (the specification of HTML 4.01 was still in transition when this document was written), then the authors' name – the World Wide Web Consortium. Following this is the DTD name and version number (4.01) and the FPI concludes with a code indicating it is written in English. Finally we have a URL linking to the DTD file.

Take note

The line which calls the DTD is sometimes called the 'document type declaration'. The document type declaration calls the document type definition! On occasion you will hear hyperlinks called URIs (Uniform Resource Identifiers). URI is the all-encompassing technical term, URL is a special case of URI governing data accessed via the Web.

Defining elements

The DTD main body consists of several component parts that define different XML structures. A DTD will mainly be composed of element definitions and attribute definitions. We may also have some code defining new entity references.

To declare an element, use the following:

```
<!ELEMENT name  (data) type>
```

The name parameter is straightforward – whatever you want to call your tag. Data can either be plain data directly for that element, or a reference to child elements. The data type is set to either **ANY** or **EMPTY**. An EMPTY element is one such as **<hr>** in HTML that contains no data. Conversely, an element with the ANY tag will accept any input as data – don't use this often as there is little point in having a DTD defining element rules that say there are no rules!

If you are defining data for the element, then the ANY and EMPTY tags are omitted (elements cannot contain data and be empty, or contain specific data and yet allow any to be used). For data, you use the term **PCDATA** with a hash in front of it:

```
<!ELEMENT myname (#PCDATA)>
```

Take note

PCDATA means 'Parsed Character Data', i.e. character strings that get sent to the parser. The word is not a reference to PC computers.

The data definition can also refer to other elements. As these are below the first element in the hierarchy, they are child elements of the parent (all XML elements apart from the root are child elements). In the following the root element (*father*) contains two required tags, *son* and *daughter*:

```
<!ELEMENT father (son, daughter)>
<!ELEMENT son (#PCDATA)>
<!ELEMENT daughter (#PCDATA)>
```

Note the comma in the root element definition. If child elements are separated by a comma, they are then required in your XML documents. What if you need an element to be optional? The solution is to use alternate elements, defined with a 'pipe' or vertical bar, rather than a comma.

```
<!ELEMENT father (son | daughter)>
<!ELEMENT son (#PCDATA)>
<!ELEMENT daughter (#PCDATA)>
```

Here you can use the elements *son* or *daughter*, but do not have to feature them both together. In some circumstances an element may require data and allow sub-elements. We say it has *mixed content*. To define mixed content, place an asterisk after the brackets containing your data definition. This line of code allows the father element to contain some text (perhaps giving the father's age) as well as the son and daughter child elements:

```
<!ELEMENT father (#PCDATA, son, daughter)*>
```

So far, so good, but what if you want an element that occurs many times inside a parent? The element **<addressbook>** could have hundreds of occurrences of the sub-element **<addressoffriend>** (assuming you have that many friends!). We need to tell the parser how many times an element is likely to occur in a document. The trick is to use an occurrence indicator. XML contains several symbols, which when added after the element name imbue it with special properties. You have already met two, the comma and the pipe symbol. An asterisk lets a child element appear zero or multiple times within a document. A plus sign declares than an element can occur one or multiple times, but it must feature at least once. A question mark lets the element occur either once or not at all.

In the element **cv**, we have to have at least one **school**, **university** can occur multiple times, but it is optional as is **jobs** (you are likely to have had more than one job in your life, but it is quite possible to have had none if you are just out of school, say):

```
<!ELEMENT cv (school+, (university | jobs)*)>
```

We have placed brackets around **university** and **jobs** so the zero or many indicator applies to both of the elements.

Take note

An asterisk inside the brackets is the indicator type for many or no occurrences. Outside the brackets it defines mixed content.

The following code contains a simple DTD definition inside an XML page, building on what we've done:

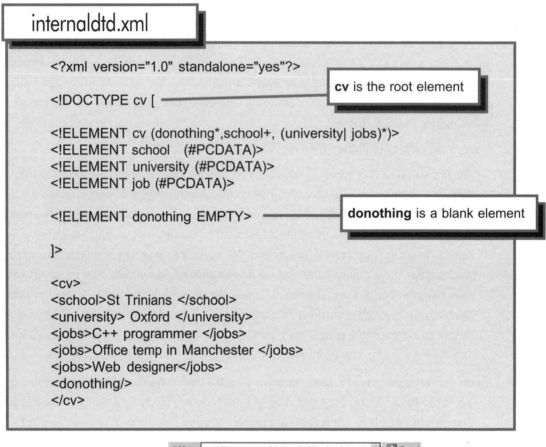

internaldtd.xml

```
<?xml version="1.0" standalone="yes"?>

<!DOCTYPE cv [                    cv is the root element

<!ELEMENT cv (donothing*,school+, (university| jobs)*)>
<!ELEMENT school   (#PCDATA)>
<!ELEMENT university (#PCDATA)>
<!ELEMENT job (#PCDATA)>

<!ELEMENT donothing EMPTY>       donothing is a blank element

]>

<cv>
<school>St Trinians </school>
<university> Oxford </university>
<jobs>C++ programmer </jobs>
<jobs>Office temp in Manchester </jobs>
<jobs>Web designer</jobs>
<donothing/>
</cv>
```

Output in Internet Explorer (DTD not displayed)

Attributes

Elements can contain attributes, so we need a system of declaring them in the document type definition. It is possible to do away with attributes altogether and place all your data in nested elements, but most programmers prefer not to, as well designed attributes can make XML pages more compact and readable.

Attributes are defined using the **ATTLIST** declaration. ATTLIST contains the handle of the element featuring the attribute, the name of the attribute, the data type and an optional default value:

```
<!ATTLIST computer ram CDATA "512 meg">
```

The element *computer* now includes an attribute *ram* specifying its memory:

```
<computer ram="256 meg">server </computer>
```

CDATA specifies character type (not to be confused with CDATA blocks in XML pages) and is one of ten allowable data types in attribute descriptions. Other types of note include **ID** (for an ID reference in the document), **NOTATION** (which we'll meet in our discussion of unparsed entities – see page 35) an **ENTITY** value and an enumerated list. Some examples:

```
<!ATTLIST computer ram CDATA "64 meg">
<!ATTLIST computer chip (Intel| AMD | PowerPC) #REQUIRED >
<!ATTLIST computer num ID >
<!ATTLIST computer flash NOTATION >
<!ATTLIST computer maths CDATA #FIXED "3.14159" >
```

We have seen the CDATA before. The second attribute, **chip**, contains an enumerated list, and the default value **REQUIRED** meaning we must include this attribute in the element. Following that is a possible **ID** number (or letter/number combination), a **NOTATION** type describing an external file type and finally an attribute with default **FIXED** value.

Take note

As well as a #REQUIRED default value, you can set an attribute to be #IMPLIED meaning it may or may not have a value, or #FIXED where the value is constant (i.e. PI 3.14159 is a numeric constant). The preceding hash is essential!

Therefore, if we have the above list of attributes, our XML document would be able to have lines like:

```
<computer ram="128 meg" chip="AMD" ID="1234" flash="comp.fla">
<computer ram="129 meg" chip="Intel" ID="1234">
<computer chip="AMD" ID="1234">
```

The following line would be invalid, as the required attribute *chip* is missing:

```
<computer ram="129 meg" ID="1234" flash="comp.fla">
```

The attribute data types can be further used to restrict the sort of information allowable in your documents. For instance, two data types we have not seen yet are **NMTOKEN** and **NMTOKENS**. These force the parser into accepting an attribute value that conforms to XML naming conventions.

If we create a user name attribute for our computer element:

```
<!ATTLIST computer username NMTOKEN>
```

the following values would be acceptable:

`<computer chip="Intel" username="Rob">`	Plain text
`<computer chip="Intel" username="Simons_comp">`	Underscore
`<computer chip="Intel" username="Sharon123">`	Numbers at end

but these would cause the document to be invalidated:

`<computer chip="Intel" username="1Rob">`	Number at start
`<computer chip="Intel" username="Simons comp">`	Contains a space

General and parameter entities

In Chapter 2 we saw how XML features several entities that allow special characters to be placed inside a document. We also saw how you can potentially insert any character by entering its code number in the entity call. XML has a function for creating your own entities – doing so can actually save you a lot of time and effort.

Having an entity define a single letter or number is important, but lacks flexibility. It would be far better if an entity could refer to a string of data, and then insert that data into the XML code wherever the entity call appears. Such a programming construct is common on other languages, and is usually known as a *macro*. User-defined XML entities have a similar function.

For instance, say you are writing a number of documents about XML and the term 'Extensible Markup Language' occurs hundreds of times. You don't really want to keep typing them out, and if you cut and paste the term that still makes the document longer than it would be if you had made your own entity. An entity will take up less space than an often-repeated string:

```
<!ENTITY xmldef "Extensible Markup Language">
```

This creates an entity called *xmldef*. If we want to use it in a document, it is preceded by an ampersand and close with a semicolon:

```
<title> The &xmldef; </title>
```

Would print "Extensible Markup Language" on your browser. Every time your XML documents have the *&xmldef;* entity, the parser replaces the entity name with the related text.

This is a *general entity* – one that is used inside an XML document. A *parameter entity* is used within the DTD itself. If we attempted to use the xmldef entity inside a DTD, an error would occur.

A parameter entity definition looks identical to a general entity reference, except for the added percentage sign. In the following example, the parameter entities define the attribute names. When there are only two attributes listed, using an entity results in a slightly longer piece of code, but imagine if a DTD contains dozens of attributes per element. This would result in some very confusing code being produced, and entities can help clarify things.

```
<!— normal definition —>
<!ELEMENT pcparts (motherboard,microprocessor)>

<!ELEMENT motherboard (#PCDATA)>
<!ELEMENT microprocessor (#PCDATA)>

<!—Definition using two parameter entities —>
<!ENTITY % main "motherboard">
<!ENTITY % cpu "microprocessor">

<!ELEMENT pcparts (%main;,%cpu)>
<!ELEMENT %main; (#PCDATA)>
<!ELEMENT %cpu (#PCDATA)>
```

Parameter entities can assume the block of text to be replaced is actually located in another file, hence it is possible to make a 'master DTD' made up of several smaller DTD documents – useful if separate teams are developing a new XML standard, say.

Tip

You can reference an external DTD by its filename and location:

`<!ENTITY parttwo SYSTEM "parttwo.dtd">`

This works for both general and parameter entities.

Unparsed entities

The third type of entity in the XML standard is the unparsed entity. An unparsed entity has a similar role to CDATA – it describes a data type the computer will skip over when it runs a particular XML document. We might want to include computer code, pictures or binary files (these could contain anything, but *binary* is generally taken to mean a file containing some data or a compiled computer program).

To define an unparsed entity two lines are needed. The first is a standard **ENTITY** keyword, but featuring the **NDATA** attribute. Following this is a **NOTATION** line explaining the file associations that exist with this entity:

```
<!ENTITY mycv "file.doc" SYSTEM NDATA worddoc>
<!ENTITY letter "letter.doc" SYSTEM NDATA worddoc>
<!NOTATION worddoc SYSTEM "msword.exe">
```

Hence in the code snippet above, the XML parser is instructed to ignore references to *mycv* and *letter*, but is told that these are a part of the unparsed datatype *worddoc*. Files referencing *worddoc* will then call *msword.exe* (thus loading them into Microsoft Word, which is correct as they are Word documents).

Take note

The **NOTATION** file-type can also be a URL or a MIME type. The MultiPurpose Internet Mail Extension system describes certain types of data on a web server. Examples of MIME types include text/html for HTML files and video/x-msvideo for AVI media files.

City guide

Based on what we know, we shall now create a DTD for a web site's XML pages. The site will be a simple city guide, containing information of interest to tourists. We are holding the DTD in an external file, so we simply list all of the element and attribute definitions, we do not need to put an XML declaration line or DOCTYPE definition (that is done later in the XML page):

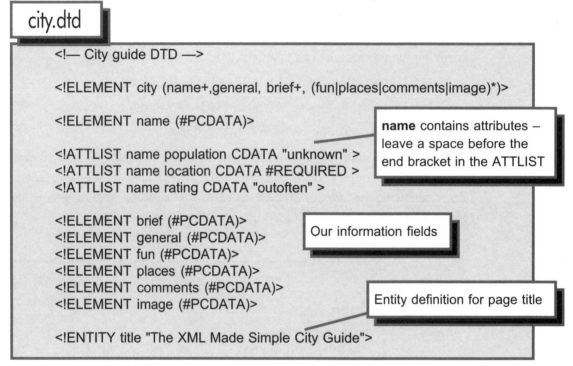

city.dtd

```
<!— City guide DTD —>

<!ELEMENT city (name+,general, brief+, (fun|places|comments|image)*)>

<!ELEMENT name (#PCDATA)>

<!ATTLIST name population CDATA "unknown" >
<!ATTLIST name location CDATA #REQUIRED >
<!ATTLIST name rating CDATA "outoften" >

<!ELEMENT brief (#PCDATA)>
<!ELEMENT general (#PCDATA)>
<!ELEMENT fun (#PCDATA)>
<!ELEMENT places (#PCDATA)>
<!ELEMENT comments (#PCDATA)>
<!ELEMENT image (#PCDATA)>

<!ENTITY title "The XML Made Simple City Guide">
```

name contains attributes – leave a space before the end bracket in the ATTLIST

Our information fields

Entity definition for page title

To get this working, we create an XML page, and reference the DTD through a DOCTYPE call:

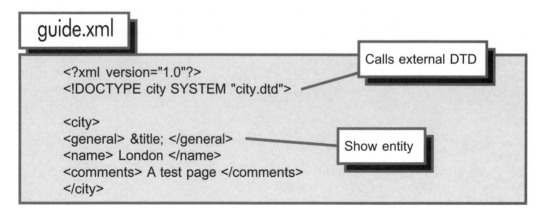

guide.xml

```
<?xml version="1.0"?>
<!DOCTYPE city SYSTEM "city.dtd">

<city>
<general> &title; </general>
<name> London </name>
<comments> A test page </comments>
</city>
```

Calls external DTD

Show entity

Running this in Internet Explorer should give us the following image, which shows how the parser has put in default attributes and the replacement text for the title entity.

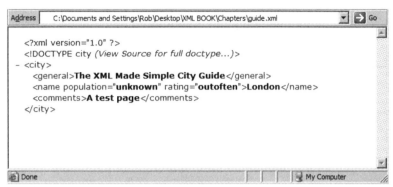

```
<?xml version="1.0" ?>
<!DOCTYPE city (View Source for full doctype...)>
- <city>
    <general>The XML Made Simple City Guide</general>
    <name population="unknown" rating="outoften">London</name>
    <comments>A test page</comments>
  </city>
```

Exercises

1   What is wrong with the following internal DTD fragment:

```
<!DOCTYPE space (

<!ELEMENT space (star*,planet+, satellite*)>
<!ELEMENT star  (#PCDATA) EMPTY>
<!ELEMENT planet (#CDATA)>
<!ELEMENT satellite (#PCDATA)>

]>
```

2   An attribute is defined by:

```
<!ATTLIST program visualbasic (ver4 | ver5 | ver6) #REQUIRED >
```

And called by:

```
<program>visualbasic</program>
```

Is this correct?

3   How would this element look in an XML file?

```
<!ELEMENT brain EMPTY>
```

4 XML on the Web

Cascading Style Sheets

So far our XML files have had the same results every time – either the page works (and you get a display of the elements or text), or it does not (and you get an error message). This is very limited. Data is described better and in a more formal way, but we need to see something interesting. Tree diagrams are not good enough!

Help is at hand – XML supports the *Cascading Style Sheet* mechanism to add aesthetic appeal to pages. CSS is a system seen widely on the Web. In the past a graphic designer would build a page for a web site with tags to describe its colours, fonts and so on. To build a similar page, much time had to be spent recoding the same set-up. Now imagine if that designer was working for a newspaper and her employers announced they wanted all of their 10,000 archive stories to have the same page design. Doing this by hand would be a nightmare. Enter Cascading Style Sheets. Now all the web designer has to do is work out the relevant look of a page and transpose this into a set of rules (titles are always be blue, hyperlinks are underlined, the background colour is white…) known as a *stylesheet*. A line referencing the stylesheet is added to each HTML page, so when that page is called the stylesheet rules take precedence and the entire site shares a consistent look.

Today, CSS is widely used by web developers although a percentage still opt for their own Heath-Robinson design solutions for page consistency (among which are using lots of tables and invisible images to act as spacers). Perhaps the reason CSS is not used by everybody is that support across browsers has been irregular. Until recently there were major inconsistencies between CSS-rendered pages. The latest generation of web browsers have considerably improved on this, so we can be fairly certain that most users will see our pages as intended.

Further driving CSS is the fact that XML uses it to help display pages. With no internal support for fonts, colours or text spacing, the XML software has to rely on external technology for providing a consistent look to pages (think of the style-sheet system as the final application of a web-based XML page).

Take note

We are now up to the CSS2 standard. Cascading Style Sheets have been around for a while (CSS appeared in 1996), but browser support has been patchy until recently.

CSS files

A Cascading Style Sheet consists of a list of style rules stored in a text file. Style rules all follow the same syntax:

    Selector {property: new value; }

The *selector* is the name of the element you wish to manipulate. The *property* describes what you are going to alter about the tag (alignment, colours, font), then after the colon you input a *new value* for the property. You can place several selectors in a group and they will all take the same rules.

    Selector1, selector2, selector3 {property: new value;}

Furthermore, CSS rules are inherited from parent to child. Hence if you have a set of nested elements, with the outside one having a style rule (for example, bold text), the elements within it will also be emboldened.

You can think of a CSS rule as something like a function block in C – all of the code is included between the two brackets. You can include as many rule calls as needed for each element as long as they are separated by semicolons (but not after the final value).

XML pages have to be able to locate the stylesheet – this is done by including a reference in the document prologue, in the following format:

    <?xml-stylesheet href= "locationofstylesheet" type="text/css" ?>

You may incorporate comments in your CSS file. A comment begins with /* and ends with */ (once again, similar to C).

    /* The next line produces large green text on a yellow background*/

Take note

Stylesheets use curly brackets { }, tags use angled brackets < > and functions like DOCTYPE use square brackets [ ]. Incorrect brackets are a typical source of syntax errors.

Our first stylesheet

Let us have some fun with a demonstration stylesheet before we look at how everything works. Type in the following XML code, then the stylesheet listing and save them together:

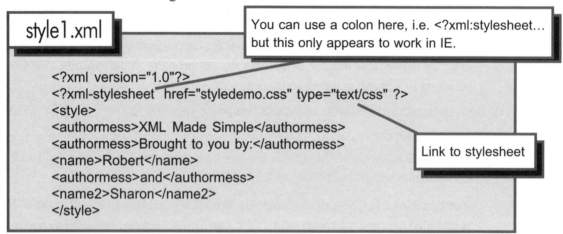

```
style1.xml
```

You can use a colon here, i.e. <?xml:stylesheet... but this only appears to work in IE.

```
<?xml version="1.0"?>
<?xml-stylesheet href="styledemo.css" type="text/css" ?>
<style>
<authormess>XML Made Simple</authormess>
<authormess>Brought to you by:</authormess>
<name>Robert</name>
<authormess>and</authormess>
<name2>Sharon</name2>
</style>
```

Link to stylesheet

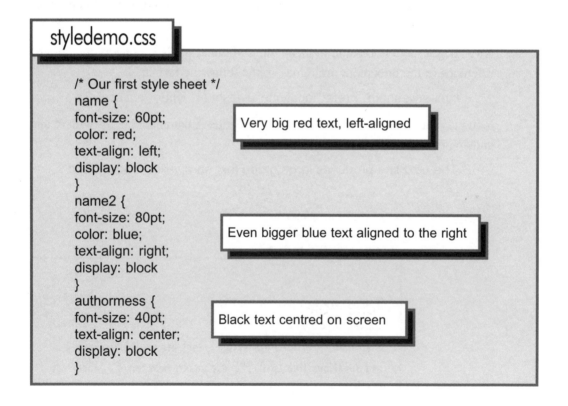

```
styledemo.css
```

```
/* Our first style sheet */
name {
font-size: 60pt;
color: red;
text-align: left;
display: block
}
name2 {
font-size: 80pt;
color: blue;
text-align: right;
display: block
}
authormess {
font-size: 40pt;
text-align: center;
display: block
}
```

Very big red text, left-aligned

Even bigger blue text aligned to the right

Black text centred on screen

If the XML is loaded without the stylesheet line, unsurprisingly the following will be seen on your monitor:

```
<?xml version="1.0" ?>
- <style>
    <authormess>XML Made Simple</authormess>
    <authormess>Brought to you by:</authormess>
    <name>Robert</name>
    <authormess>and</authormess>
    <name2>Sharon</name2>
  </style>
```

But with the stylesheet engaged everything changes:

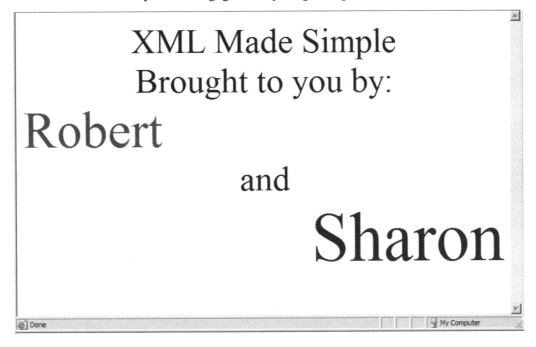

Now we have to look at the stylesheet in more detail to see what we have done. There are three element blocks, corresponding to separate tags in the XML code, which set four aspects of the text's appearance.

The first element property, **font-size**, seems straightforward, a value for the size of a font. We are using the default font and order the browser to display this in 80 point text, and as there are 72 points to the inch, the text should be just over an inch high on your screen. This is not always the case as monitor screens can vary in precision. Hence we could an alternate measurement scale. The stylesheet accepts measurements in inches (in) and centimetres (cm), or for the most computer-relevant measurement you can specify the size in pixels (px). If you don't wish to use a unit of measurement, CSS will accept a size word (*small*, *medium*, *large*, *x-large*) or a percentage value ("150%").

The **color** property can be set by giving its hexadecimal RGB value, or using a standard colour name.

The **text-align** property sets the alignment of the whole paragraph, and can be left, right or centre.

The **display** property describes how a portion of text should be shown. The default value is *inline*, meaning there are no newline characters between chunks of text. Setting the value to *block* adds a new line before and after the element data, thus breaking up text on screen. Setting display's value to *none* actually makes the entire element block disappear.

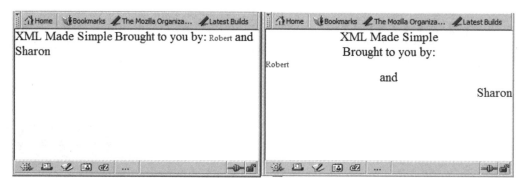

Mozilla browser views with display value set to *inline* and *block*

Tip
———
There's a comprehensive guide to CSS in HTML 4.0 Made Simple.

44

Text features

Colour codes in a style-sheet is identical to their HTML cousins. The most popular colours can be referred to by name (*yellow*, *blue*, *cyan*) or by a hexadecimal number, based on the relative intensities of red, green and blue.

Use **color** for text colour, and **background-color** for the background. (Note the US spelling of 'colour'.) Also note that **background-color** only alters the colour in the selected block of text – and not the colour of the entire screen, unless told to.

To set text in bold, use **font-weight** either with the description *bold*, or a value from 100-900 (normal text at 400, darkest text at 900).

Setting the font is done via the **font-family** property. You can specify the font name, but you can't be sure a specific font will be installed on all the computers that visit your page, and sometimes a font is called by a slightly different name on other platforms. If the font name has spaces, enclose the name in quotes.

The inbuilt CSS **font-family** values are *serif*, *san-serif*, *cursive*, *fantasy* and *monospace*. Access them with a property call like this:

```
Tagname {font-family: "Arial Black", Helvetica, san-serif}
```

This example offers two fonts by name, but if they are both unavailable on the displaying browser, it asks for the local san-serif font to be used.

text-decoration is the property included to add effects such as underlining or strike-through to element data. The **text-transform** property is used to alter the case of a block of text. Values can be *uppercase*, *lowercase*, *capitalize* and *none*.

This snippet of code incorporates what we've learned to alter the properties of the author message block. Delete the old *authormess* selector from *styledemo.css* and type the code in. You will see that the main text font has changed, the text has turned red, become underlined, and it is placed on a somewhat garish yellow background:

```
authormess {
font-family: {"Arial Black", san-serif};
font-weight: 400;
font-size: 20px;
text-align: center;
color: red;
background-color: yellow;
text-decoration: underline;
display:block
}
```

More style

If pretty colours were all you could do with CSS, it would not have attained such popularity in the web development world. CSS also has properties for altering the way text is positioned on screen. The **letter-spacing** property takes a value (in points, pixels, inches, etc.) and places a space of that size between individual letters. Similarly, **word-spacing** controls the spacing between entire words.

Every HTML programmer knows how annoying it is trying to format text correctly. One particular problem lies in the spacing between lines. You can do away with line problems of this type in CSS. The **line-height** property determines the distance between lines of text. It is even possible to let text overlap vertically by setting the value of line-height to one or two pixels, although this is not really recommended because many browsers have trouble displaying the result correctly.

All of the text you see on screen actually exists in a rectangular box that stays invisible unless you put a border around it. We can control the box by setting its margins using the CSS properties **margin-left**, **margin-right**, **margin-top** and **margin-bottom**. To draw a border around the box we use the **border** element together with a thickness, border type and colour value.

This listing demonstrates these points. Again, we have an XML file and a stylesheet.

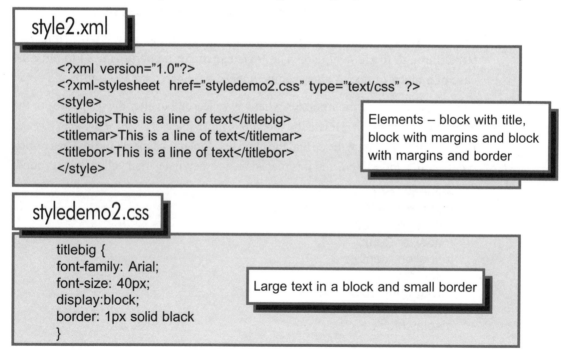

style2.xml

```
<?xml version="1.0"?>
<?xml-stylesheet  href="styledemo2.css" type="text/css" ?>
<style>
<titlebig>This is a line of text</titlebig>
<titlemar>This is a line of text</titlemar>
<titlebor>This is a line of text</titlebor>
</style>
```

Elements – block with title, block with margins and block with margins and border

styledemo2.css

```
titlebig {
font-family: Arial;
font-size: 40px;
display:block;
border: 1px solid black
}
```

Large text in a block and small border

46

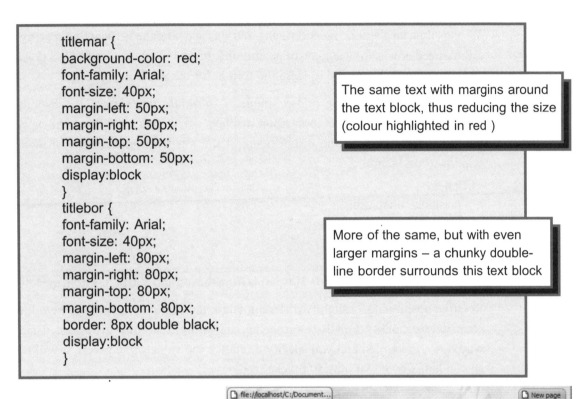

```
titlemar {
background-color: red;
font-family: Arial;
font-size: 40px;
margin-left: 50px;
margin-right: 50px;
margin-top: 50px;
margin-bottom: 50px;
display:block
}
titlebor {
font-family: Arial;
font-size: 40px;
margin-left: 80px;
margin-right: 80px;
margin-top: 80px;
margin-bottom: 80px;
border: 8px double black;
display:block
}
```

The same text with margins around the text block, thus reducing the size (colour highlighted in red)

More of the same, but with even larger margins – a chunky double-line border surrounds this text block

Program output in Opera

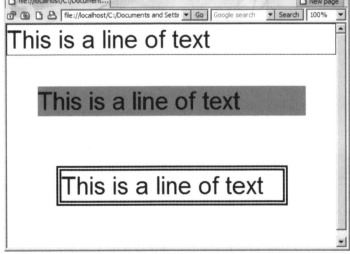

As you can see, a text block without a margin (outlined by the single pixel border) takes up the entire width of the browser window. Our second block has 50 pixel margins around it. In the third element the margins have grown to 80 pixels each – the chunky border demonstrates how much the final text box has shrunk.

Positioning elements

We can align an element, indent it using margins and alter the vertical line spacing. All we need now is for a method of positioning the text block on screen. CSS gives us this ability, but we need to learn the format for the position property.

Position can work in one of two modes – *absolute* or *relative*. In absolute positioning, the stylesheet processor displays an element block at the x, y coordinates given, with the origin being at the top left corner of the browser window. For example:

```
Text {
position: absolute;
Left: 200px;
Top: 100px
}
```

This will place the element box 100 pixels from the top and 200 pixels from the left.

Relative positioning is slightly different. Here, the origin is the place where the element box should normally be displayed, so if your text is going to be printed half way down the screen and you specify a relative top value of 50 pixels, it will be shown half way down plus 50 pixels:

```
Text {
position: relative;
Left: 10px;
Top: 50px
}
```

These final listings show how to use positioning to create working overlay effects. We have created two elements, **<pres>** which shows the word 'Presenting', and **<title>** for our book title. The stylesheet sets our words up in large fonts, then positions them in the browser window such that the title is clearly in front.

Take note

Be very careful when positioning elements. You can never be sure what sort of screen sizes people are likely to use and any display created with absolute positioning might fail miserably on a large percentage of browsers.

```
<?xml version="1.0"?>
<?xml-stylesheet  href="styledemo3.css" type="text/css" ?>
<style>
<pres>PRESENTING</pres>
<title>XML MADE SIMPLE</title>
</style>
```

```
title {
font-family: Arial;
font-size: 60px;
color: blue;
position: absolute; left: 30px; top: 40px;
}
pres {
font-family: Arial;
font-size: 48px;
word-spacing: 20px;
color: red;
position: absolute; left:160px; top: 16px;
}
```

Title text shown in large blue font

Presenting element text shown in a smaller font and starting 160 pixels from the left and 16 from the top

Text overlapping effect with CSS

Exercises

1   What would happen to an XML document if there are errors in the stylesheet?

2   The CSS property **background-image** allows us to incorporate a picture behind a text block. For example, we load a picture of Edinburgh with the property:

background-image: url("edinburgh.jpg");

This image is placed in the background of the element box. A further property **background-repeat** lets us tessellate the image across the screen (setting the value to *repeat*), tile it across the x or y-axis (*repeat-x*, *repeat-y*), or leave the image static (*no-repeat*). With this information, make a simple collage of pictures using CSS and a basic XML file.

3   Design a page using the elements in the city-guide DTD described in the last chapter. Use a stylesheet to create an attractive display.

5 Namespaces and XSD

Namespaces

The freedom XML gives programmers to create their own markup is extremely useful, but what if two parties wish to share data and have tags with identical names, but different meanings?

Both of the basic XML documents shown here include the root element **<media>**, although one is referring to digital media file formats and the other describes news organisations. A way is required of separating out identically named elements that hold different types of data. We have this problem in the real-world (for instance American and British English have a small percentage of identical words with different meanings) and it exists with computers, too.

```
<?xml version="1.0"?>
<media>
<format> Flash </format>
<format> mp3 </format>
</media>
```

```
<?xml version="1.0"?>
<media>
<news> The Guardian </news>
<news> BBC One </news>
</media>
```

To solve the predicament, XML provides you with **namespace** facilities. A namespace is a way of identifying elements within an XML document, and consists of a pointer to the namespace and an identifying prefix. The prefix is then placed in front of all tags where a possible clash could occur.

Namespace syntax

The syntax for setting up your own namespace involves placing a line with the following parameters in the XML prologue:

```
<element xmlns: prefix= "aspecificURL">
```

The XML parser does not really bother to see if the URL you enter is valid. The whole idea is that each URL is unique, so that can be used as an ID for each namespace. Of course this does not mean you can use other people's web-site addresses for your own namespace without permission!

The majority of namespace users will actually place a real web-page at the address specified in the namespace element. If you are writing XML code that is going to be used by other people, it is best to make sure that your namespace declarations point to a web-site you have control over.

To use namespaces with the above code, we must incorporate the namespace definitions and the new prefixes to each tag. In the example we have called the prefixes *com* and *ne* for news:

```
<?xml version="1.0"?>
<cm:media  xmlns:cm="http:somecomputersiteplace.com">
<cm:format> Flash </cm:format>
<cm:format> mp3 </cm:format>
</cm:media>
```

```
<?xml version="1.0"?>
<ne:media  xmlns:ne="www.anewssite.co.uk">
<ne:news> The Guardian </ne:news>
<ne:news> BBC One </ne:news>
</ne:media>
```

We can make the prefixes as short as possible – even single-letter prefixes would be fine for many applications. Make sure you don't add an extra space before the prefix, and also that you do not call the prefix *xml* as this will confuse the parser and result in your pages being not well-formed.

If you omit the prefix from the declaration the computer will set up a default namespace. In the example below, we have removed the *cm* prefix from our file format code – the elements are all now associated with the namespace identified by the "http:somecomputersiteplace.com" URL.

```
<?xml version="1.0"?>
<media xmlns="http:somecomputersiteplace.com">
<format> Flash </format>
<format> mp3 </format>
</media>
```

This makes the code easier to read and saves on typing. We can have more than one namespace operating on a single document, or apply namespaces to attributes. In the following code the two *format* elements mean different things (once again, the first *format* is for digital files and the second for paper sizes), but they have different namespaces so the parser treats them as separate.

```
<?xml version="1.0"?>
<cm:media xmlns:cm="http://www.stuff.co.uk"
xmlns:dm="http://www.test.com">
<cm:format> Flash </cm:format>
<cm:format> mp3 </cm:format>
<dm:format> A4 </dm:format>
<dm:format> A3 </dm:format>
</cm:media>
```

If the *cm* prefix is removed, this is treated as the default document namespace, but with the *dm* elements still being marked, the parser behaves as before:

```
<?xml version="1.0"?>
<media xmlns="http://www.stuff.co.uk"
xmlns:dm="http://www.test.com">
<format> Flash </format>
<format> mp3 </format>
<dm:format> A4 </dm:format>
<dm:format> A3 </dm:format>
</media>
```

Default namespace applied to **media** root tag and all its elements unless otherwise specified

dm calls second namespace for these tags

We can see that namespaces are an excellent way of avoiding conflicts between element names. A further use of namespaces is to tell the computer when an XML document contains elements related to another XML language, such as XSD.

XSD

To ensure document validity the XML programmer will place a set of rules inside a Document Type Definition. The DTD system has several shortcomings – files are written in a format different to plain XML and there are limitations on how data is described. Something else was needed to handle the more complex XML applications being created – for example if you are dealing with files on a database you will want control over data types (letters, numbers, dates), values and string lengths – a basic DTD cannot do these things.

Enter the XML Schema language, known commonly as the **XML Schema Definition** or XSD. As with DTDs an XSD file describes what elements and attributes are valid in an XML file. XSD is itself written in XML, which means a schema can be processed by the parser alongside the XML documents that refer to it. As the language is written in XML the parser will determine if the code is well-formed. This can help eliminate many common syntax errors.

A Schema uses namespaces to differentiate itself from standard XML. To use a schema in your documents, place a link to its namespaces inside the root element.

In computer science a schema *refers to a description of how data is organised and structured. Outside of XSD, the word is frequently used in database terminology to describe a document or diagrams that show exactly how the elements of the database interact with each other.*

Schema1.xml

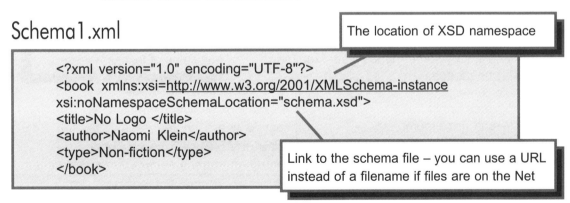

The location of XSD namespace

```
<?xml version="1.0" encoding="UTF-8"?>
<book  xmlns:xsi=http://www.w3.org/2001/XMLSchema-instance
xsi:noNamespaceSchemaLocation="schema.xsd">
<title>No Logo </title>
<author>Naomi  Klein</author>
<type>Non-fiction</type>
</book>
```

Link to the schema file – you can use a URL instead of a filename if files are on the Net

Looking at the XML listing above you will notice the namespace additions to the **<book>** element. The first one is the location of the XMLSchema namespace at W3C. The second namespace is a little more complicated. When referencing a Schema you use the **SchemaLocation** attribute together with a target namespace and a location (URL or filename). These are example legal values for the location.

xsi:schemaLocation="http://www.mynamespace.com note.xsd"

xsi:schemaLocation="http://www.mynamespace.com
www.mynamespace.com/note.xsd"

The target namespace ensures that your schema does not conflict with any others. In the examples in this chapter the files are located on your own PC so there is no real need for a discrete namespace. Therefore the *schemaLocation* file is prefixed with the words **noNamespace**, and the file *schema1.xml* is looking for a XSD file called *schema.xsd*.

schema.xsd

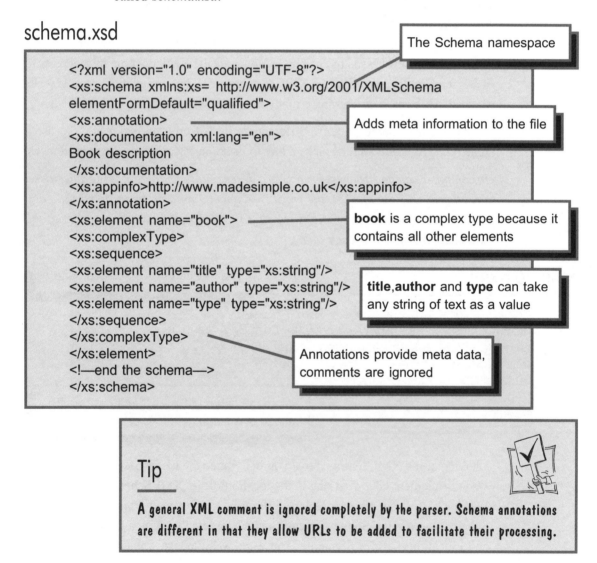

A XSD document begins with an XML declaration followed by the namespace definition. Any prefix can be used to refer to the elements, but here we have stuck with **xs**, as many programmers use this by default for schemas (although **xsd** is popular in some quarters). The optional **elementFormDefault** attribute is generally set to "qualified" if you are dealing with complex data types (see later).

We have placed an **<annotation>** element at the beginning of the XSD code. Programmers use annotation to add commentary to their schemas. The intention is to provide extra information either to programmers or computers interpreting the documents. The **<documentation>** element contains general comments on the whole document and a language attribute (in this case ENglish), **<appinfo>** is designed for providing information to computer programs that use the schema. Both **appinfo** and **documentation** will accept a link or text as element data.

Take note

In many XML applications element names are written in a mixture of upper and lower case. You must use exactly the same upper/lower case combination as the parser will not recognise the elements otherwise. For instance if 'complexType' is entered as 'complextype' a validation error will result.

Element types

Elements in XSD can be thought of as simple or complex data types. A simple element type is one where the element contains text and does not allow any sub-elements. A complex element type can have attributes, nested elements or be empty. For example if you were to define HTML using an XML schema **<head>** would be complex because the header can contain several elements (i.e. **<title>** or **<meta>**). The **<title>** element is a simple type as that will only contain a string representing the name of the web page.

The process of building your own schema is similar to that of defining a DTD – work out what elements you wish to use in your documents, ascertain what attributes they have and how the elements are laid out, then build an XSD file containing this information. In the file *schema1.xml* we can see that the root element is called **<book>**, and so must be defined as a complex type. A complex type contains the element name, the **complextype** element and a **<sequence>** of simple element types:

```
<xs:element name="elementname">
<xs:complexType>
<xs:sequence>
<xs:element name="taga" type="xs:string"/>
<xs:element name="tagb" type="xs:string"/>
</xs:sequence>
</xs:complexType>
</xs:element>
```

<sequence> is an XSD indicator. These are an enhanced version of occurrence indicators in a DTD. If it is used the elements must follow the order they are defined in. In our example, a book will have a title, author and type. If you put **title** after **type** or some other permutation, the document is declared invalid. If you prefer to have elements in any order, use the indicator **<all>** instead. If you require a choice between elements, **<choice>** lets you choose between them.

XSD has two special occurrence indicators (**maxOccurs** and **minOccurs**) that tell the parser how many times a specific element may be included inside a document. By default **minOccurs** is set to 1, meaning an element may appear at least once in a document. Setting **minOccurs** to 0 makes an element optional. The **maxOccurs** attribute sets the maximum amount of times an element can feature inside a single document. Setting **maxOccurs** to "*unbounded*" allows the element to occur as often as you like.

These example definitions show the occurrence indicators more clearly.

```
<xs:element name="optional" type="xs:string" minOccurs="0"/>
```

```
<xs:element name="nm" type="xs:string" minOccurs="1"
maxOccurs="40"/>
```

```
<xs:element name="maxfive" type="xs:string" maxOccurs="5"/>
```

```
<xs:element name="infinite" type="xs:string" maxOccurs="unbounded"/>
```

Data types

A simple element contains the element name followed by a data type, and an optional indicator attribute. XSD comes into its own here by having an extensive list of valid data types. If you have ever used a powerful database system such as MySQL or Oracle you will know that many different types of data are allowed (the same goes for programming languages). If data types are used carefully any software packages that handle large amounts of information will be able to process it far more efficiently.

Our examples so far have only used string types, but XSD can do far more and accept data in dozens of different string and numerical formats, the most common being string, time, date, URI (a type of URL), integer & decimal numbers, binary and Boolean (on/off) data.

Example Data Type	Possible values within element
type="xs:string"	Character string, e.g. "Hello there!"
type="xs:decimal"	A decimal number, e.g. 11.6, 5.3
type="xs:integer"	A whole number, e.g. 7,8,42
type="xs:anyURI"	A site link, e.g. www.yahoo.co.uk
type="xs:date"	Year/Month/Day, e.g. 2003-08-15
type="xs:time"	Hour/Min/Sec, e.g. 10:22:00
type="xs:duration"	PeriodYrMnthHrMinSec, e.g. P4Y3M2D
type="xs:byte"	8 bit value from −128 to 127
type="xs:negativeInteger"	Negative whole number, e.g. -256
type="xs:nonNegativeInteger"	Positive whole number, e.g. 100,999
type="xs:boolean"	TRUE,FALSE, 1 or 0

After selecting a data type you may specify a default value which the element is initialised to. You can in addition set a fixed value that cannot be changed.

```
<xs:element name="month" type="xs:string" default="Jan"/>
<xs:element name="pi" type="xs:decimal" fixed="3.14159"/>
```

Facets

You can create your own simple data types and program each one to restrict the sort of data it will accept as valid. To do this, start with the name as an attribute of the **simpleType** element, follow with the **restriction** (sometimes called 'facet') **base** (containing the data type) and one or more allowable values.

This shows a simple facet:

```
<xs:simpleType name="restrict">
<xs:restriction base="xs:string">
<xs:maxLength value="4"/>
</xs:restriction>
</xs:simpletype>
```

To call the new datatype, we reference the name (without the namespace prefix) inside a new simple element definition:

```
<xs:element name="type" type="restrict"/>
```

As you can probably tell, this example code allows an element called "*type*" which is made from the new restrict data type. The element may take a string of up to and including four characters in length – any more will produce a validation error.

Facet types

For a string data type you can set the **maxLength** and **minLength** values by using their relevant elements. In the restrict code we could easily have set **minLength** to 4, meaning the element content has to be at least four letters long. If you want a series of possible values (for instance radio programme categories) a list is built using enumerated values:

```
<xs:enumeration value="Entertainment"/>
<xs:enumeration value="News"/>
<xs:enumeration value="Sport"/>
<xs:enumeration value="Music"/>
```

For numerical values, a typical facet would set the **minInclusive** or **maxInclusive** values. The **minInclusive** is a value higher than or equal to x, where x is the element data. Similarly **maxInclusive** covers numbers going up to and including x. You will use these to set an acceptable range, e.g. for a number between 50 and 200

```
<xs:minInclusive value="50"/>
<xs:maxInclusive value="200"/>
```

Using **totalDigits** lets the computer know the maximum allowable length of a number, **fractionDigits** states how many decimal places are allowed

```
<xs:totalDigits value="7"/>        A number up to seven digits long.
<xs:fractionDigits value="2"/>     Number 1.55 is valid, 1.552 is not.
```

You may further restrict allowable numbers by using what is called a restriction pattern. These are similar to the input masks you see in databases.

Of the patterns below, the first lets the element allow alphabetical characters or numbers. There must be between 4 and 8 characters in the string. The second pattern allows lower case letters only and the element data has to be 5 characters long. The third pattern looks for an element value consisting of at least 4 digits and finally we are looking for a one to four character long string containing numbers or letters from A-F – hence this would be a perfect filter for a hexadecimal number (a four character hex number holds values up to 65535):

```
<xs:pattern  value="[a-zA-Z0-9]{4,8}"/>
<xs:pattern  value="[a-z]{5}"/>
<xs:pattern  value="(\d){4,}"/>
<xs:pattern  value="[a-fA-F0-9]{1,4}"/>
```

On a final note, the whitespace in a string value can also be restricted. You may set **whitespace** to *preserve* the spacing, *replace* (changes characters such as line feeds to a space) or *collapse* (multiple spaces are reduced to a single space as in HTML).

```
<xs:whiteSpace value="preserve"/>  "Space   text" stays unaltered
<xs:whiteSpace value="collapse"/>  "Space   text" turns to "Space text"
```

Take note

Inclusive includes the target number. XSD permits you to use an Exclusive value where the acceptable value is one more or less than the limit, e.g. to only accept a number between 51 and 199:

```
<xs:minExclusive value="50"/>
<xs:maxExclusive value="200"/>
```

Attributes

An attribute can be thought of as another simple data type, and is defined using the attribute element. Each attribute definition should include the name and data type. You may add optional attributes – a default value and a use value. The use attribute tells the parser whether a particular attribute is optional (default) or required. The following are examples of valid attribute definitions:

```
<xs:attribute name="code" type="xs:number" use="optional"/>
<xs:attribute name="colour" type="xs:string" use="optional"/>
<xs:attribute name="id" type="xs:string" use="required"/>
```

Both attributes and elements can be grouped for later use. It is common to place attributes and data restrictions inside a simpleContent element. The code below defines a group called *att*, containing an *age* number and book *titles* string attribute. The attribute group is called inside the data type by using the **ref** keyword. You can use ref to call elements or attributes in other parts of the schema.

```
<xs:attributeGroup name="att">
<xs:attribute name="age" type="xs:number"/>
<xs:attribute name="titles" type="xs:string"/>
</xs:attributeGroup>

<xs:element name="author">
<xs:complexType>
<xs:simpleContent>
<xs:extension base="xs:string">
<xs:attributeGroup ref="att"/>
</xs:extension>
</xs:simpleContent>
</xs:complexType>
</xs:element>
```

A new schema

With what we have learned up to now we can create a final demonstration schema to show how everything works. The file *bio.xml* is linked to a schema which makes sure the *name*, *employment* and *skills* elements are included, restricts the age of the person to within a valid range and allows the empty element **<online/>** without causing a validation error.

bio.xml

```
<?xml version="1.0" encoding="UTF-8"?>
<bio xmlns:xsi="http://www.w3.org/2001/XMLSchema-instance"
xsi:noNamespaceSchemaLocation="bio.xsd">
<name age="31">M.Jones</name>
<employment>Stuntperson</employment>
<skills>Parachuting</skills>
<skills>Martial arts</skills>
<skills>Stunt driving</skills>
<hobbies>Base jumping, sky diving</hobbies>
<online/>
</bio>
```

hobbies and **online** elements are optional, the others are mandatory

Bio.xsd

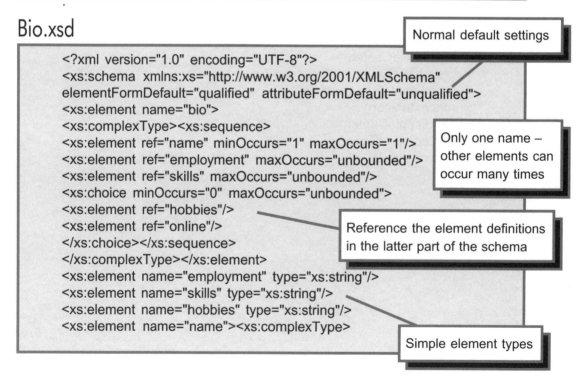

Normal default settings

```
<?xml version="1.0" encoding="UTF-8"?>
<xs:schema xmlns:xs="http://www.w3.org/2001/XMLSchema"
elementFormDefault="qualified" attributeFormDefault="unqualified">
<xs:element name="bio">
<xs:complexType><xs:sequence>
<xs:element ref="name" minOccurs="1" maxOccurs="1"/>
<xs:element ref="employment" maxOccurs="unbounded"/>
<xs:element ref="skills" maxOccurs="unbounded"/>
<xs:choice minOccurs="0" maxOccurs="unbounded">
<xs:element ref="hobbies"/>
<xs:element ref="online"/>
</xs:choice></xs:sequence>
</xs:complexType></xs:element>
<xs:element name="employment" type="xs:string"/>
<xs:element name="skills" type="xs:string"/>
<xs:element name="hobbies" type="xs:string"/>
<xs:element name="name"><xs:complexType>
```

Only one name – other elements can occur many times

Reference the element definitions in the latter part of the schema

Simple element types

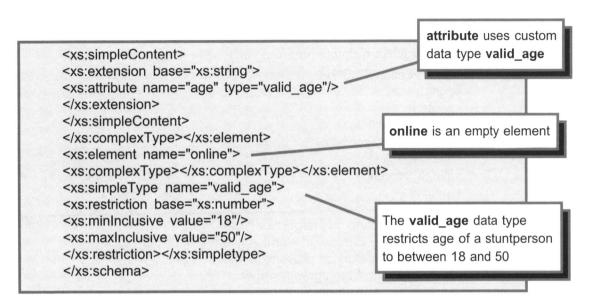

```
<xs:simpleContent>
<xs:extension base="xs:string">
<xs:attribute name="age" type="valid_age"/>
</xs:extension>
</xs:simpleContent>
</xs:complexType></xs:element>
<xs:element name="online">
<xs:complexType></xs:complexType></xs:element>
<xs:simpleType name="valid_age">
<xs:restriction base="xs:number">
<xs:minInclusive value="18"/>
<xs:maxInclusive value="50"/>
</xs:restriction></xs:simpletype>
</xs:schema>
```

attribute uses custom data type **valid_age**

online is an empty element

The **valid_age** data type restricts age of a stuntperson to between 18 and 50

This concludes our brief sojourn into XML Schemas. The XSD language is very comprehensive, so this introduction has focussed on the main functions a programmer has to know to make their own schemas and to read other peoples. XSD will eventually replace Document Type Definitions because of its improved flexibility and data handling functions. There already exists software that can make the process of schema creation easier, and even convert a DTD into an XSD file.

Tip

The commercial XML Spy editor (http://www.xmlspy.com/) has a utility for converting DTDs to Schemas and schema construction facilities (see Chapter 10). Visit the W3C schema tools page at: http://www.w3.org/XML/Schema for useful utilities including DTD to XSD converter programs.

Exercises

1 There is a problem with this code, can you resolve it using namespaces?

```xml
<?xml version="1.0"?>
<compsec>
<people>
<title>Doctor</title>
<title>Professor</title>
<title>Mr</title>
<title>Miss</title>
</people>
<papers>
<title>New security vulnerabilities</title>
<title>Stopping Computer Worms</title>
<title>Denial of Service prevention</title>
<title>Quantum Cryptography</title>
</papers>
</compsec>
```

2 Why would you use the XML Schema language instead of a DTD?

3 Create your own schema for the city guide, as a possible DTD replacement.

6 XSLT

Transforming XML

The **Extensible Stylesheet Language** (XSL) is the most powerful component of the XML family, and consists of three software technologies that turn XML elements into other forms. XSL is a very powerful document processing system, and we can only hope to touch on some introductory concepts here.

We are using XSL transforms on a client machine to demonstrate the basic principles. In reality, most of the XSL processing is done on *servers*. Earlier we mentioned how a hypothetical organisation might like to turn its data into many different formats. In the not-so-distant past, converting from one electronic format to another was a difficult and costly business. With XML and XSL such conversion becomes financially viable, as the processes are done automatically. You can have a single set of documents held in XML format, then convert them as needed for a plethora of uses.

Server-side document conversion has other advantages; as you can never be sure what kinds of applications people are running, it makes sense to send them pre-processed data. Imagine a web server that sent pure XML documents to clients. People running one of the latest browsers could read the pages as intended. Those unfortunates who used older browsers without the necessary XML engine would find themselves looking at screenfuls of gibberish.

On the other hand, if the XML is converted to HTML on the browser (or even XHTML) pretty much everybody could view the documents. One might image a business creating several types of converted HTML documents for specific browser families. When a user made contact with the company's web servers, their browser type would be read, and this information used to redirect them automatically to the appropriate pages. There is no reason why this process could not go further with the server making customised web pages for mobile devices. Everything would derive from the original XML documents, which would be sitting in a data archive completely unaltered.

XML is an excellent way of storing and describing data, XSL turns that data into usable form. The part of XSL that does the conversion is called XSLT (eXtensible Stylesheet Language Transformation) which works on the basis of templates. A *template* contains a piece of information that should match with identical information in the source documents. When a match occurs the template has further instructions on what operations to perform on the matched data.

Transformations on the client

To experiment with XSL, the procedure is similar to the one you used with CSS – create your XML file and your stylesheet and reference the stylesheet in the XML. Unfortunately not all browsers have XSL capabilities built in. Internet Explorer versions 5 and above are fine as the Microsoft XML parser has an XSL engine. Mozilla can handle XSL documents fairly well. Opera tends to ignore the XSL stylesheet, so you are left with the plain text of your otherwise well-formed XML.

Type in these XML and XSL files, and load the XML file into a browser.

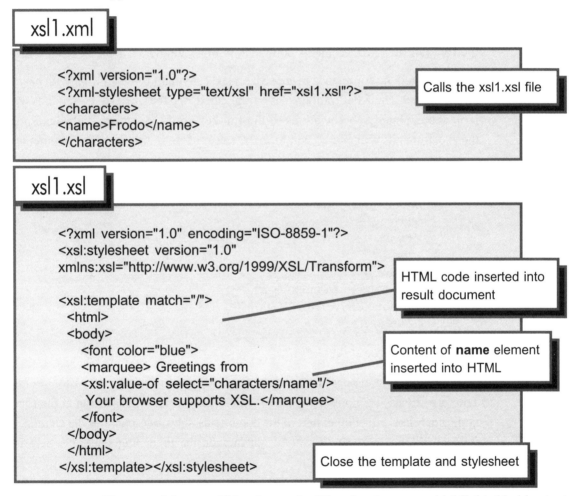

xsl1.xml

```
<?xml version="1.0"?>
<?xml-stylesheet type="text/xsl" href="xsl1.xsl"?>
<characters>
<name>Frodo</name>
</characters>
```

Calls the xsl1.xsl file

xsl1.xsl

```
<?xml version="1.0" encoding="ISO-8859-1"?>
<xsl:stylesheet version="1.0"
xmlns:xsl="http://www.w3.org/1999/XSL/Transform">

<xsl:template match="/">
  <html>
  <body>
    <font color="blue">
    <marquee> Greetings from
    <xsl:value-of select="characters/name"/>
     Your browser supports XSL.</marquee>
    </font>
  </body>
  </html>
</xsl:template></xsl:stylesheet>
```

HTML code inserted into result document

Content of **name** element inserted into HTML

Close the template and stylesheet

If successful, you will be shown the 'Greetings' message highlighted in blue text (it scrolls as well if viewed on Internet Explorer). If not, you will simply see a name displayed – or nothing at all.

XPath

Computer systems store files in directories (also called 'folders'), which may be visualised as another type of tree structure, with a 'root' directory at the top of the tree. To reference a file, you describe its position by reference to its directory (the nodes of the tree) and the filename, which together make its 'path name'. Hence on a Windows system a file might be located at *C:\Program Files\Myprograms*.

With XSL code, rather than simply finding a document (which is done via its URI) you often want to access parent and child elements within it. We can do this with the XPath language which can navigate a path through the document tree. XPath recognises several types of nodes such as the document (entire XML document), the root (all the XML elements contained within), elements, attributes and text.

To understand the commands in an XSL stylesheet you must be familiar with basic XPath syntax. The XPath language is complicated, and the subset of commands we look at are actually abbreviations of the full keywords. However, understanding these commands will enable you to make sense of most simple XSL documents.

Some XML code for illustration of XPath expressions.

```
<root>
   <one>
      <two/>
      <two/>
      <three>
         <two/>
         <monday weather="rain""/>
         <tuesday weather="snow"/>
      </three>
   </one>
</root>
```

To access the root element in this document, we would use the expression **/root**. The forward slash denotes an absolute path to the element (i.e. starting at the root node, not relative to another part of the document), the slash separates the elements (nodes) in the document. If you do not include the preceding slash, the path is relative to the current element:

/root/one	Select the <one> element
one/two	Relative jump from <one> to <two> element
/root/one/two	Select the child element <two>
/root/one/three/two	Select child element <two> inside <three> element

An attribute is described by using the @ symbol. A comparison expression may be placed in square brackets to find a particular element whose attribute value matches the search:

root/one/three/Monday/@weather   Select the weather attribute

root/one/three/Monday[@weather= 'rain']   Select element with 'rain' value

Using a double forward slash selects all of the elements in a document with the desired name, irrespective of their location:

//@weather   Selects weather attributes

//two   Selects all the <two> elements

The star symbol is used to represent wildcard elements (as in file handling). A wildcard is used in place of an element name:

/root/one/three/*   Selects elements located between the tags named <three>

//*   Select all of the elements in the document

The period or dot (.) refers to the current element; two of them (..) denote the parent element in a parent/child relationship:

/root/.   Refers to the root element

/root/one/three/.. <one> is the parent element of <three>

If a document has a series of identical elements in a list, we can add an index number in square brackets to specify the desired element:

/root/one/two[1]   First <two> element in list

/root/one/two[2]   Second <two> element

/root/one/two[last()] Final <two> element

Take note

If you view a XSL transformed document in your web browser, you will notice that the error messages are sometimes inaccurate. The code may be missing a closing tag in the XSLT line, but the browser reports an error somewhere else. This is common among programming language error-checkers, and one reason why programs are not always easy to debug.

Making a XSLT stylesheet

We can now build a simple XSLT stylesheet and put some of our new XPath knowledge into practice. Type in the following two documents and load the XML document into your browser.

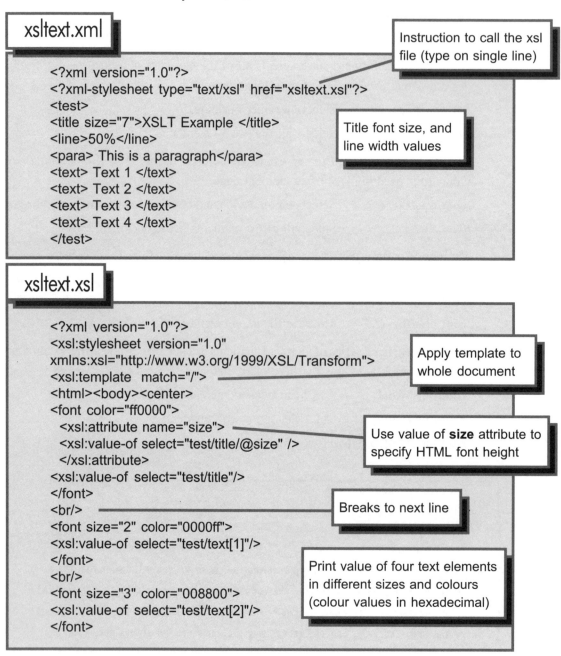

xsltext.xml

```
<?xml version="1.0"?>
<?xml-stylesheet type="text/xsl" href="xsltext.xsl"?>
<test>
<title size="7">XSLT Example </title>
<line>50%</line>
<para> This is a paragraph</para>
<text> Text 1 </text>
<text> Text 2 </text>
<text> Text 3 </text>
<text> Text 4 </text>
</test>
```

Instruction to call the xsl file (type on single line)

Title font size, and line width values

xsltext.xsl

```
<?xml version="1.0"?>
<xsl:stylesheet version="1.0"
xmlns:xsl="http://www.w3.org/1999/XSL/Transform">
<xsl:template  match="/">
<html><body><center>
<font color="ff0000">
  <xsl:attribute name="size">
  <xsl:value-of select="test/title/@size" />
  </xsl:attribute>
<xsl:value-of select="test/title"/>
</font>
<br/>
<font size="2" color="0000ff">
<xsl:value-of select="test/text[1]"/>
</font>
<br/>
<font size="3" color="008800">
<xsl:value-of select="test/text[2]"/>
</font>
```

Apply template to whole document

Use value of **size** attribute to specify HTML font height

Breaks to next line

Print value of four text elements in different sizes and colours (colour values in hexadecimal)

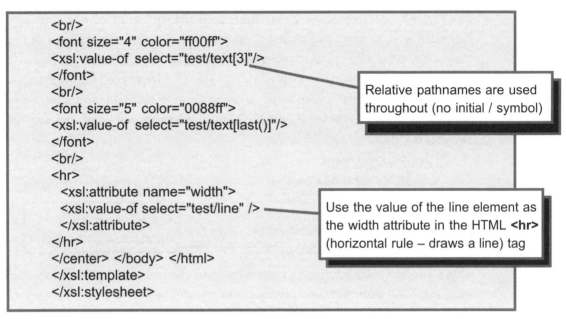

```
<br/>
<font size="4" color="ff00ff">
<xsl:value-of select="test/text[3]"/>
</font>
<br/>
<font size="5" color="0088ff">
<xsl:value-of select="test/text[last()]"/>
</font>
<br/>
<hr>
  <xsl:attribute name="width">
  <xsl:value-of select="test/line" />
  </xsl:attribute>
</hr>
</center> </body> </html>
</xsl:template>
</xsl:stylesheet>
```

Relative pathnames are used throughout (no initial / symbol)

Use the value of the line element as the width attribute in the HTML **\<hr\>** (horizontal rule – draws a line) tag

If all goes well, you should see the following display on your browser:

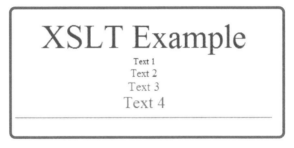

The XSLT code is a mixture of XSLT commands containing XPath expressions. At the start we define the XSLT namespace, then open a template. This applies to the entire document. Following on are some HTML commands, so we know the output is going to be HTML, rather than WML or another markup language.

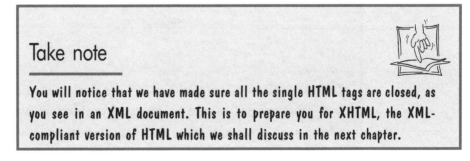

Take note

You will notice that we have made sure all the single HTML tags are closed, as you see in an XML document. This is to prepare you for XHTML, the XML-compliant version of HTML which we shall discuss in the next chapter.

The first few XSL lines show the **attribute** command in use. In markup languages you often need to transform an XML value to the value of a tag attribute. If you simply place the value in the document an error will result. The correct way is to start with the target element (in this case, the HTML **<font>**) and follow that with an **attribute** command whose value is the name of the attribute to be set. Next, **value-of select** draws the value from the XPath expression, and finally the attribute element is closed.

```
<font color="ff0000">
  <xsl:attribute name="size">
  <xsl:value-of select="test/title/@size" />
  </xsl:attribute>
<xsl:value-of select="test/title"/>
</font>
```

Close elements after an attribute conversion

This stylesheet code gets the **size** attribute value (@ indicates an attribute value) from the XML document and places it into a font size attribute in the converted page. The content string of the title element is printed, and finally the font element is correctly closed. The code translates in HTML to:

```
<font color="ff0000" size="7">
XSLT Example
</font>
```

The next sets of lines insert the values of the first, second, third and final **<text>** values into HTML **<font>** tags and prints them out, each in a different colour.

Finally, we use **attribute** once more. This time the value of the XML **<line>** element is inserted into the **width** attribute of a **<hr>** tag, thus drawing a horizontal line 50% of the screen width on your browser window.

To check that the stylesheet really is inserting the values from the XML code, you may like to change the values for **size** and **<line>** around and see what happens.

Tip

You can use **attribute** to insert a picture into a document. Store the filename in an XML element, then when you program your stylesheet insert the filename value into an <img src="filename"/> tag using similar code to that shown above.

Multiple templates

We should say a few more words about template at this point. Through this chapter, we are using a single root template to convert text in the documents. This approach works for short documents, but would become unwieldy for longer ones. XSLT allows programmers to use as many templates as they wish, with a few provisos. Templates must be nested with one template calling another. This is done by having your template code, and at the point you wish another template to be placed, include an apply-templates element. The computer then passes to the next template included in the document. This brief example shows how:

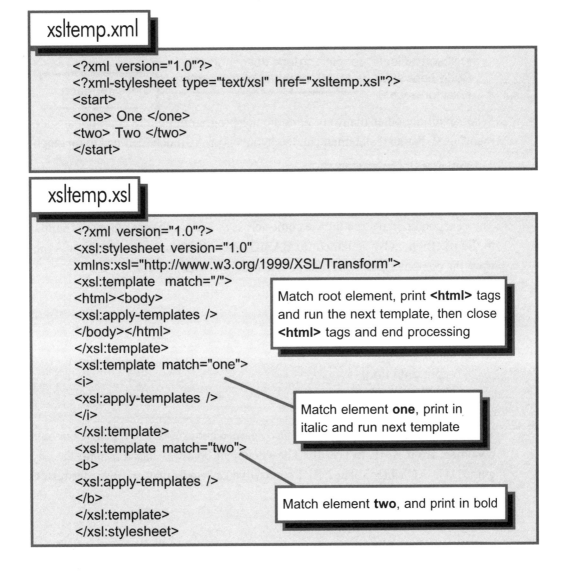

xsltemp.xml

```
<?xml version="1.0"?>
<?xml-stylesheet type="text/xsl" href="xsltemp.xsl"?>
<start>
<one> One </one>
<two> Two </two>
</start>
```

xsltemp.xsl

```
<?xml version="1.0"?>
<xsl:stylesheet version="1.0"
xmlns:xsl="http://www.w3.org/1999/XSL/Transform">
<xsl:template match="/">
<html><body>
<xsl:apply-templates />
</body></html>
</xsl:template>
<xsl:template match="one">
<i>
<xsl:apply-templates />
</i>
</xsl:template>
<xsl:template match="two">
<b>
<xsl:apply-templates />
</b>
</xsl:template>
</xsl:stylesheet>
```

Match root element, print **<html>** tags and run the next template, then close **<html>** tags and end processing

Match element **one**, print in italic and run next template

Match element **two**, and print in bold

Looping and checking

Using **value-of select** with an XPath string allows you to pull any element from an XML document and insert it into a new transform file. However, **value-of** will on its own merely fetch the first matching element. In the stylesheet we had four separate value-of calls to display the four elements. We did this because each output varies in the HTML document. What if you want to print out a series of elements in your result code? If you have a table with 100 values, it is inconceivable you would sit there typing the same lines again and again. XSLT has full looping facilities – using the **for-each** command – which obviate the need to do this.

A loop in XSLT must be structured correctly, closing the **for-each** at the end.

```
<xsl:for-each select="characters/names">
<xsl:sort select="people" order="descending"/>
Code here such as HTML or value-of elements
</xsl:for-each>
```
Close **for-each**

What about the other mainstay of computer programming, the conditional statement? XSL has an **if** statement, and its syntax is pretty much identical to **for-each**:

```
<xsl:if test="somestring">
output data here
</xsl:if>
```

The next conditional structure we come across in XSL is **choose**. **choose** is similar to the **if…then…else** statement in BASIC where **if** a particular condition is met **then** the computer performs a task, **else** it does something else.

```
<xsl:choose>
  <xsl:when test="somestring">
    output data here
  </xsl:when>
  <xsl:otherwise>
   output data here
  </xsl:otherwise>
</xsl:choose>
```

We can now use the information we have learned about XSLT to translate our own document from XML to HTML. The document below is based around the city guide DTD in Chapter 3. The XSLT code will take data from it, and place the results into a HTML table.

```
<?xml version="1.0"?>
<?xml-stylesheet type="text/xsl" href="xsl2.xsl"?>
<!DOCTYPE city SYSTEM "city.dtd">
<city>
<name location="uk">
<brief>Liverpool is in the North of England.</brief>
<general>Three universities, two cathedrals, one airport </general>
<fun>Bars, clubs, the FACT center</fun>
<places>Albert Dock</places>
<places>Speke Hall</places>
<places>The Cathedrals</places>
<comments>An interesting place - Jim</comments>
<comments>Scary! - Beaker</comments>
<comments>Good fun if you like to party - Sally</comments>
</name>
</city>
```

> Stylesheet and reference the DTD from Chapter 3 (this must be in same folder)

```
<?xml version="1.0"?>
<xsl:stylesheet version="1.0"
xmlns:xsl="http://www.w3.org/1999/XSL/Transform">
<xsl:template match="/">
<html><body>

<xsl:if test="//name[@location='uk']">
<font size="2"><i>UK version </i></font>
</xsl:if>
<hr width="60%" align="left"/>
<!-- HTML table -->
<table border="0">
<tr><th>Category</th><th>Info</th></tr>
<tr><td><font color="0000ff">Brief Description:</font> </td>
<td><xsl:value-of select="//brief"/></td></tr>
<tr><td><font color="0000ff">General info:</font> </td>
<td><xsl:value-of select="//general"/></td></tr>
<tr><td><font color="0000ff">Fun bits:</font> </td>
<td><xsl:value-of select="//fun"/></td></tr>
```

> If location is 'uk' print "UK Version"

> HTML table with border and **<th>** header.

> Only one **brief** – so // will display all (i.e one) instances of it – same for **general** and **fun**

```
<tr><td><font color="0000ff">Places to Visit:</font></td></tr>
<xsl:for-each select="city/name/places">
<xsl:sort select="places" order="descending" data-type="text"/>
<tr><td></td> <td>
<xsl:value-of select="."/>
</td></tr>
</xsl:for-each>
<tr><td><font color="0000ff">Your Comments:</font></td></tr>
<xsl:for-each select="city/name/comments">
<xsl:sort select="comments" order="ascending"/>
<tr><td></td> <td>
<xsl:value-of select="."/>
</td></tr>
</xsl:for-each>
</table>
<hr width="60%" align="left"/>
<xsl:choose>
<xsl:when test="count(/city/name/comments)>2">
<font size="2"> Page popularity: High </font>
</xsl:when>
<xsl:otherwise>
<font size="2"> Page popularity: Average </font>
</xsl:otherwise>
</xsl:choose>
</body></html>
</xsl:template>
</xsl:stylesheet>
```

Optional **data-type** can be text or number

Count number of **<comments>** , if over 2 print the 'High' , else print 'Average' – count expressions must be absolute (note preceding slash)

Screenshot showing text inside table

UK version

Category	Info
Brief Description:	Liverpool is in the North of England.
General info:	Three universities, two cathedrals, one airport
Fun bits:	Bars, clubs, the FACT center
Places to Visit:	
	Albert Dock
	Speke Hall
	The Cathedrals
Your Comments:	
	An interesting place - Jim
	Scary! - Beaker
	Good fun if you like to party - Sally

Page popularity: High

78

Near to the start of the stylesheet, the **if** statement checks to see if the **location** attribute of **<name>** is set to "uk" and if so prints out a message.

The main output is placed inside a HTML table. You will encounter an almost identical table mechanism on WML pages (see Chapter 8), only WML tables are slightly simpler and have some required attributes.

Printing the contents of multiple elements is done using a **for-each** loop:

```
<xsl:for-each select="city/name/places">
<xsl:sort select="places" order="descending" data-type="text"/>
<tr><td></td> <td>
<xsl:value-of select="."/>
</td></tr>
</xsl:for-each>
```

Remember the closing / on sort and value-of

The program navigates to the path shown by the relative XPath in the first line, then sorts the results of the selected element (**<places>**) into descending order and prints the output text in the second cell of a two cell row (the first being for the headings). The **value-of** element seems almost blank, but the period is the XPath abbreviation for the current element. Hence the loop says, "Go to city/names/places then print the current <places> text, and loop until all the matching elements are shown".

At the end of the code is another comparison block – this time **choose**. In the test, the **count** operator adds the number of nodes returned by an XPath expression. Hence this counts the <comments> elements – of which there are three (**count** adds them up – if you are using numeric data, **sum** will give you the total of the values).

The check for greater than two uses the traditional > symbol. XPath allows mathematical expressions to be evaluated using the symbols common to most computer languages, so the following would all be perfectly legal expressions:

```
<xsl:when test="count(/city/name/comments)>(1+2)">
```

Greater than 3?

```
<xsl:when test="count(/city/name/comments)<20">
```

Less than 20?

```
<xsl:when test="count(/city/name/comments)>=5">
```

Greater than or equal to 5?

Exercises

1   Explain why XSLT is a more powerful technology than CSS.

2   What advantages are there in transforming documents on the server, rather than the client? Could you think of a possible disadvantage?

3   Use XSL to produce an enhanced HTML page using the city guide DTD. Instead of duplicating the approach used in this chapter, try and make your page more colourful, better formatted and include a picture of your town at the bottom.

Take note

If your browser cannot resolve XSL code, you can download a third-party XSLT system, such as James Clarks' XT. This is available for free download from the web site:

     http://www.blnz.com/xt/index.html

As XT is written in Java, versions should work on any platform with a Java Virtual Machine. The program is started from the command prompt, and accepts three filenames as input – the XML code, the stylesheet and a destination for the result, e.g.

     xt xsl1.xml xsl1.xsl xsltest.htm

To use the new file, load it into your web browser.

7 XML miscellany

Linking

So far our XML pages are static – we have not come across a standard way in XML to link between files. You will not be surprised to learn that there is a separate XML language devoted to this very topic. Originally called the XML Linking Language, it has since branched off into two separate (but related) standards, **XLink** for linking to documents and **XPointer** for locating information within documents. However, XLink isn't about merely using URLs to connect to other files, it is built to allow complex interlinks between documents.

XLink has support for simple linking (similar to what happens in web pages) and a more in-depth system where you can connect to multiple sources. A simple link consists of the link element followed by a short series of attributes. We start with the element namespace, followed by the URL – held in an identical format to HTML. Following this are several attributes whose purposes are somewhat atypical for a hyperlinking process:

Role creates an identifier for this document on the network

Title the title text to display somewhere in the browser when you move your pointing device over the link.

Show has two options, **replace** loads the page in the current browser window and **new** will open another window for the linked document.

Actuate can be set to either activate the link when you first enter a page (*onLoad*), or when you click on the link (*onRequest*).

This piece of code creates our first XML hyperlink. We are only giving an example of the simple linking capabilities as they are the only ones with at least a small amount of browser support:

```
<?xml version="1.0"?>
<media xmlns:xlink="http://www.w3.org/1999/xlink" >
<xlink:hyperlink xlink:type="simple"
xlink:href="http://www.google.com"
xlink:title="Search for things"
xlink:role="Search ID"
xlink:show="new"
xlink:actuate="onRequest">Go Googling</xlink:hyperlink>
</media>
```

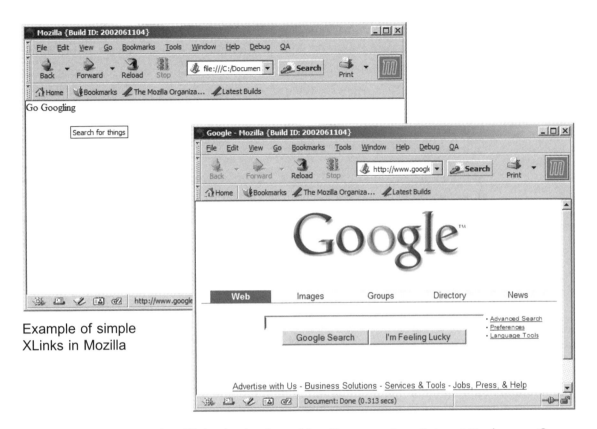

Example of simple
XLinks in Mozilla

This code will do absolutely nothing if you run it on Internet Explorer or Opera. It does work correctly in Mozilla and some versions of the Netscape browser. As the images show, the XLink shows the text in the title attribute when you pass the mouse over it (also called a tool-tip). If you click on the link, the result is opened in a new browser window.

Take note

Mozilla is based on a publicly-released version of Netscape's source code. As such both browsers are much alike. There are now variants using the more modern Mozilla engine, like Firebird available for free download (for Mac, Windows and Linux) from: http://www.mozilla.org/products/firebird/

The idea behind **XPointer** is that an XPointer program can scan through a document looking for specific links and retrieve the most relevant information, based on a series of element matches. This sounds similar to HTML anchors, but with XPointer the concept is stretched to the limit. For example you would be able to point to a web-site and find a particular piece of data, then retrieve only that data. At present all you can do is fetch an entire page. XPointer holds out a lot of promise, though certain technical issues have to be overcome before it is in widespread use.

At the moment XLink support is minimal on browsers. The XPointer standard has almost no browser support at all. Both standards were formalised in 2001, so are likely to be implemented on the next generation of web browser applications. For the next few years at least you should be wary about using XLink code on your XML sites.

XHTML

You may have seen the term XHTML used in discussions about the Internet and are wondering what it means. **Extensible Hypertext Markup Language** is designed to overcome some of the shortcomings of HTML and in structure is basically HTML 4.01 reconfigured as an XML application. In day-to-day use XHMTL is effectively identical with HTML, but it has been designed to be more efficient and follow the strict grammatical rules of XML. Hence XHTML is likely to be the most popular XML-based language in use for the foreseeable future.

Creating web pages using XML means they can be validated and checked for errors, but the XML syntax can be confusing to many people who don't have a programming background. Because of the similarities with generic HTML, web designers can therefore create pages in XHTML without having to learn anything about XML syntax (as long as they follow the few rules we speak about in a moment). Well-formed XHTML has the advantage of being future-proofed for the next generation of Internet applications while still having the ability to work on current, and many of the older browsers.

Having XHTML as the standard for web documents should make it easier to implement on less powerful hardware. It is expected that eventually more people will access the Internet via mobile phones and related wireless devices than will use personal computers. Presently these devices mainly use WAP (Wireless Application Protocol – see Chapter 9) markup, but in the near future a single document standard would allow one set of data to be viewed on a multitude of devices with little or no modification. By using XHTML, programmers can create a compact XML browser to interpret the code, thus allowing the creation of high-quality browser programs for mobile devices.

Tip

Dreamweaver MX has an inbuilt document conversion system. If you load up a HTML file, then select File > Convert > XHTML, the program will make your page compliant in a fraction of a second. If you want a free utility to convert your pages, try HTML Tidy (http://tidy.sourceforge.net/) — there are versions for the Macintosh and various flavours of Unix.

Converting HTML to XHTML

Eventually XHTML will replace HTML, so you should be aware of how to make your documents compatible. Generally you have to follow a few rules that are identical to the XML grammar rules we introduced earlier.

- All opening tags must have a closing tag – omitting one will result in an error.

- Single tags like **\<hr\>** should also close, but there should be a space between the tag name and the closing mark: **\<hr /\>**.

- All tags must be written in lower-case. XML is case-sensitive, but HTML isn't.

- Attributes values should be surrounded by single or double quote marks.

- Elements should be properly nested.

The best way to compare HTML and XHTML is to have a look at a single piece of code. First of all, we have the code written in HTML, complete with various faux pas, such as missing tags and multiple cases used in elements:

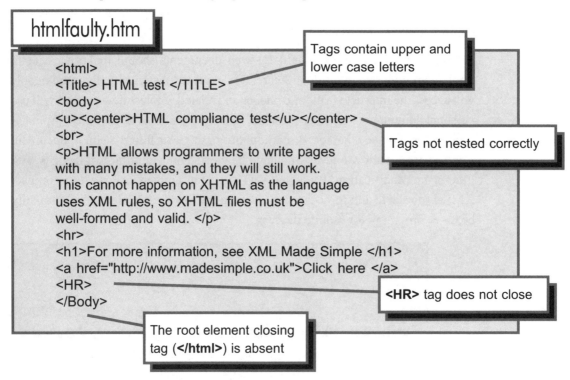

```
htmlfaulty.htm

<html>
<Title> HTML test </TITLE>
<body>
<u><center>HTML compliance test</u></center>
<br>
<p>HTML allows programmers to write pages
with many mistakes, and they will still work.
This cannot happen on XHTML as the language
uses XML rules, so XHTML files must be
well-formed and valid. </p>
<hr>
<h1>For more information, see XML Made Simple </h1>
<a href="http://www.madesimple.co.uk">Click here </a>
<HR>
</Body>
```

Tags contain upper and lower case letters

Tags not nested correctly

\<HR\> tag does not close

The root element closing tag (**\</html\>**) is absent

Converting the text to XHTML is a matter of fixing the HTML errors, and then placing an XML prologue at the top of the page. For very small bits of code it is straightforward to do the conversion yourself. If you are converting hundreds (or even thousands of documents) you will need a conversion program to help you.

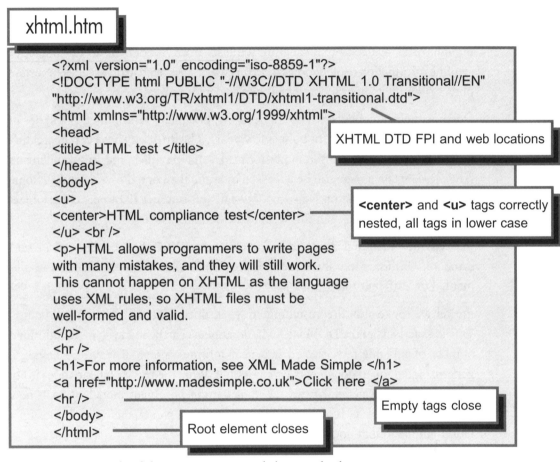

xhtml.htm

```
<?xml version="1.0" encoding="iso-8859-1"?>
<!DOCTYPE html PUBLIC "-//W3C//DTD XHTML 1.0 Transitional//EN"
"http://www.w3.org/TR/xhtml1/DTD/xhtml1-transitional.dtd">
<html xmlns="http://www.w3.org/1999/xhtml">
<head>
<title> HTML test </title>
</head>
<body>
<u
<center>HTML compliance test</center>
</u> <br />
<p>HTML allows programmers to write pages
with many mistakes, and they will still work.
This cannot happen on XHTML as the language
uses XML rules, so XHTML files must be
well-formed and valid.
</p>
<hr />
<h1>For more information, see XML Made Simple </h1>
<a href="http://www.madesimple.co.uk">Click here </a>
<hr />
</body>
</html>
```

XHTML DTD FPI and web locations

<center> and **<u>** tags correctly nested, all tags in lower case

Empty tags close

Root element closes

Both of these programs result in exactly the same output.

HTML compliance test

HTML allows programmers to write pages with many mistakes, and they will still work. This cannot happen on XHTML as the language uses XML rules, so XHTML files must be well-formed and valid.

For more information, see XML Made Simple

Click here

Done   My Computer

Document object models

So far we have seen how software packages take XML code and do something useful with it. How does an application program communicate with an XML page? Instead of thinking of the XML as a list of elements, it can be envisioned using an object model. With an object system, a unit of data (and perhaps code) can be thought of as a black box accepting requests from the outside to do things, or sending information to other objects. In this way all we need to do to access a certain object is know its identity and what parameters it will take.

Document object models, where an electronic document is described as a series of objects have been around for quite a few years. The difficulty has been in creating a unified model across different platforms. Even today there are still problems in how elements on a page can be accessed by more than one browser family. Some object code works fine on Netscape, but fails on Internet Explorer. Other object code will be fine on IE, but fail when executed on Opera.

In XML the situation is different as from the outset XML had to adhere to a DOM standard. Unfortunately there are still problems in how exactly DOM is implemented on different platforms.

Earlier we spoke about representing an XML document via a tree data structure. This is exactly what the DOM is! XML documents can be made up of an unlimited number of possible tags, nested in a near-infinite variety of ways, so having a generic model for all documents is impossible. What the DOM standard does is lay down how to use general rules for constructing an object model of each new document. When a XML document is run through a parser, the parser builds up a DOM unique to that document.

We begin with the root element (document element in DOM parlance) at the top of the DOM. From this other elements and attributes branch off – we call these *nodes*. A node is represented by a code number, which refers to the data type held within it. When a programmer wants to write an XML application, they will be able to send commands to do things such as read element data from the DOM, check values, delete elements or add new ones. While at a basic level DOM is fine for programming tasks, it can get very complicated when dealing with large documents. Imagine trying to visualise the document model for an XML file containing hundreds (or even thousands) of elements. With DOM you have a lot of power to manipulate XML, but actually using that power can be extremely difficult.

SAX

Nevertheless, the DOM is not the only way to communicate with XML elements. Another popular system is SAX (Simple API for XML). SAX was originally released as an addition to the Java language, although SAX support is now available for C++, Pascal and PERL among others.

SAX works in a different way. Instead of building the entire tree at once, you work with the document structure a part at a time. When something important happens (you reach the end of the document, say) a message is sent to your application. By interpreting the different messages and acting on them you can work on the XML.

To illustrate the two approaches, imagine if you had a large XML file containing the names of all the people in a town. You wish to find a Miss Adams. Adams is likely to be close to the beginning of the file and so a SAX-based application would quickly find it. Meanwhile, the DOM application would first have to build a tree that includes all the people from A–Z. It may take a tiny instant of time to locate the right node containing Miss Adams's information, but overall the process is not that efficient. Of course if you needed to find thousands of names, the DOM system would win out because it could access the entire data tree at once after it has been built.

Take note

An Applications Programming Interface is a library of code that system programmers make available in order to make their applications or devices easier to write software for. Using an API stops you from having to start from scratch every time you write new programs, as common coding requests are made using the API.

Tip

For a full technical overview of SAX, visit: http://www.saxproject.org/
For similar coverage of the XML DOM, go to: http://www.w3.org/DOM/

Exercises

1   Create simple XLink code to link to external sites on the city guide page. For example, in the links element you could connect to the council, or the tourist board.

2   Can you see a possible serious problem with the **xlink:actuate** attribute?

3   The following piece of XHTML prints a table on screen with data inside it. Can you find the mistakes which stop the code from being well-formed?

```
<?xml version="1.0" encoding="iso-8859-1"?>
<!DOCTYPE html PUBLIC "-//W3C//DTD XHTML 1.0 Transitional//EN"
"http://www.w3.org/TR/xhtml1/DTD/xhtml1-transitional.dtd">
<html xmlns="http://www.w3.org/1999/xhtml">
<head>
<title>Books</title>
<meta http-equiv="Content-Type" content="text/html;charset=iso-8859-1" />
</head>
<body>
<p align="center"><strong><font color="#0000CC">Classic 1990s Science
Fiction</font></strong></p>
<table width="430" border="0" align="center">
  <tr>
    <td><strong>Title</td></strong></td>
    <td><strong>Author</strong></td>
  </tr>
  <tr>
    <td><font colour="#003366">Mars Trilogy</font></td>
    <td><font color="#FF0000">Kim Stanley Robinson</font></td>
  </tr>
  <tr>
    <td><font color="#003366">Cryptonomicon</font></td>
    <td><font color="#FF0000">Neal Stephenson</font></td>
  </tr>
  <tr>
    <td><font color="#003366>Idoru</font></td>
    <td><font color="#FF0000>William Gibson</font></td>
  </tr>
  <tr>
    <td><font colour="#003366>Darwin's Radio</font></td>
    <td><font color="#FF0000>Greg Bear</font></td>
  </tr>
</table>
</body>
</xml>
```

8 Enhancing Web content

Multimedia

Perhaps the application which drives computer technology the most today is multimedia. The integration of sound, still images and video can be seen everywhere from computer games to movies. Multimedia on the Internet has tended to be slightly hit and miss over the years. Support for images and simple animations (using GIF pictures) has been around since the mid-1990s. Nowadays, stylesheets let designers build better-looking pages, and most web browsers allow the use of plug-in programs to increase functionality.

The problem with all this is that there is no single standard governing how we incorporate media data into web pages. Macromedia's Flash player is installed on millions of machines, but Flash is a proprietary system and not a part of the markup language of the browser. Ideally we need an extension to HTML which lets us view multimedia and will work on different platforms.

Creating a markup language for multimedia means having two sets of commands; commands to display data in different formats and commands to synchronise this data with a timing mechanism. General HTML has no inbuilt timing facilities (interestingly WML on mobile devices – which we will meet in the next chapter – does, along with HTML + Time incorporated into Internet Explorer) leaving programmers to create their own solutions – for example by the use of JavaScript code to alter page elements at specific intervals, or to communicate with a multimedia plug-in like RealPlayer or Flash.

Take note

Microsoft have incorporated a system called HTML + Time to directly handle multimedia content in the browser. HTML + Time is based on the latest version of SMIL (see the next section). For more information visit:

http://msdn.microsoft.com/library/default.asp?url=/workshop/author/behaviors/time.asp

SMIL

The good news is that an XML-based multimedia language has existed for a while. *SMIL* (Synchronized Multimedia Integration Language) is built on the framework of an earlier multimedia software architecture called HyTime.

SMIL is pronounced 'smile' and is presently up to version 2.0. See the W3C audiovisual pages for more details: http://www.w3.org/AudioVideo/

Sadly, SMIL is not supported consistently on the major web browsing platforms, which has led to its popularity being limited compared to other technologies. Content publishers are more likely to use Flash or embedded PowerPoint files for their presentations, but little by little the situation is changing. SMIL has definite advantages over commercial multimedia creation languages – not least being you can create SMIL with a text editor and a free player, thus saving you a lot of money on software!

Overview of SMIL

For testing SMIL pages you will need an appropriate media player program. RealNetworks' **RealOne** player has good SMIL support, and we will be using it to test the SMIL files created in this part of the book. If you have **QuickTime** installed on your computer, you can also use the player program to run your SMIL presentations, although there might be minor differences in the way some elements are displayed.

Making a SMIL file is easy – enter your source code in a text editor and save it onto disk with the file extension **.SMIL** (or **.SMI**).

Take note

A free basic version of RealPlayer is available for Windows, Apple and Unix platforms from www.real.com

QuickTime's gratis player for Mac or Windows can be downloaded from Apple's site at: http://www.apple.com/quicktime/download/

Your first SMIL file

To start you off, type in the following listing. For this to work you will need to save a couple of JPEG images (called *ukimage1.jpg* and *ukimage2.jpg*) in the same folder as the code.

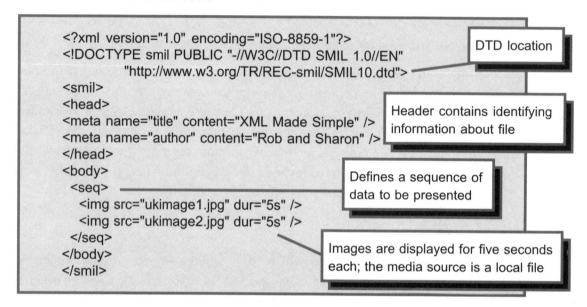

```
<?xml version="1.0" encoding="ISO-8859-1"?>
<!DOCTYPE smil PUBLIC "-//W3C//DTD SMIL 1.0//EN"
          "http://www.w3.org/TR/REC-smil/SMIL10.dtd">
<smil>
<head>
<meta name="title" content="XML Made Simple" />
<meta name="author" content="Rob and Sharon" />
</head>
<body>
  <seq>
    <img src="ukimage1.jpg" dur="5s" />
    <img src="ukimage2.jpg" dur="5s" />
  </seq>
</body>
</smil>
```

DTD location

Header contains identifying information about file

Defines a sequence of data to be presented

Images are displayed for five seconds each; the media source is a local file

SMIL looks suspiciously like HTML. While the root element is the **<smil>** tag, the document contains a head with meta information and a body that holds the main code. In this example two images are loaded one after the other – in SMIL all media elements are called via their URLs (even text is stored in external files). In the examples we give, the files called are held locally, but the source could be anywhere on the Internet with an address like "www.locationofmedia.com/mediafiles/pic.jpg".

To run this program, load it into RealPlayer or Quicktime. If you have problems reported (i.e. RealPlayer giving a 'general error'), remove the XML prologue. SMIL is slightly different to the other XML technologies we've looked at – if you do not add a DTD link to the top of the file, the SMIL player will assume that a version 1.0 SMIL presentation is running and won't give an error. The aim in this section is really to introduce the main elements of SMIL so we do not need the advanced animation capabilities of version 2.0. Therefore from now on the remaining demo files are not shown with the **xml** and **DOCTYPE** lines, and will be adhering to SMIL 1.0.

The listing contains some meta-information that helps identify it to users. If you want to see this data in full, then select the clip properties option in RealPlayer (use the command **File** > **Clip Properties** > **View Clip Info**).

Media tags have a whole list of attributes that let the file creator apply meta information to them, be it a title, author details or even an abstract of the presentation. It is perfectly legal to use tags like this in your pages:

```
<video src="city.mpeg" title="Video grab of town center" author="Rob"/>
```

Looking at the code closer, we can see the **<seq>** tag with the image links inside it. Anything inside a **<seq>** block is played in sequence a set number of times. Having a system for playing elements linearly is useful but for attractive presentations we need to be able to mix elements and get them to run at the same time. As the name Synchronized Multimedia Integration Language suggests, synchronising media elements is a core function.

Rich media

To let multiple media play together we use the **<par>** element. Media between the **<par>** tags will run simultaneously, e.g. a video with a synchronised audio track.

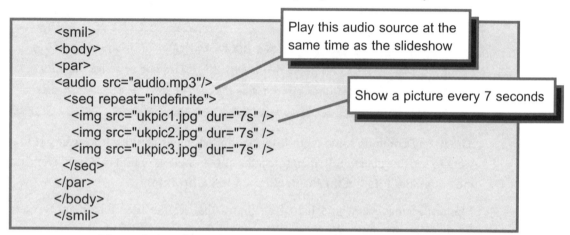

```
<smil>
<body>
<par>
<audio src="audio.mp3"/>
  <seq repeat="indefinite">
    <img src="ukpic1.jpg" dur="7s" />
    <img src="ukpic2.jpg" dur="7s" />
    <img src="ukpic3.jpg" dur="7s" />
  </seq>
</par>
</body>
</smil>
```

> Play this audio source at the same time as the slideshow

> Show a picture every 7 seconds

The code is self-explanatory – three pictures are shown and audio (music or a commentary) plays in the background. The slideshow should take 21 seconds to cycle through, if the audio is that length or shorter. If you include parallel media the presentation will not finish until the parallel source finishes. You can use the **begin** attribute to set a delay before a media element starts. If the audio in our code was 25 seconds long, we might insert a delay in the **img tag** of four seconds:

```
<img src="ukpic1.jpg" begin="4s" dur="7s" />
```

The audio will then play on its own for a bit until the slideshow starts. The **repeat** attribute can be given an integer value if you want a sequence to play a set number of times (setting it to 2 in the above example would loop the pictures twice).

If you run the above code on RealPlayer the screen may go haywire – the player itself will display the pictures with a large amount of black space and misalign them. This brings us to another important part of SMIL – regions.

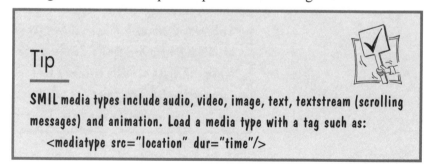

Tip

SMIL media types include audio, video, image, text, textstream (scrolling messages) and animation. Load a media type with a tag such as:

```
<mediatype src="location" dur="time"/>
```

Regions

When you create a multimedia presentation everything takes place on the main layout screen (effectively the display window of your player). SMIL allows programmers to split this window up into any number of user-defined regions, and dispatch different content to each region.

To set up regions, first of all you need to have a **layout** parent element. Within this you define the **root-layout** (the size of the entire display), followed by one or more **region** tags. The regions are given unique id names, so later on when we want to display media in a particular area, all we have to do is include a reference to the region name within our media tags.

This listing sets up a two-region display, one area for still images and one for text:

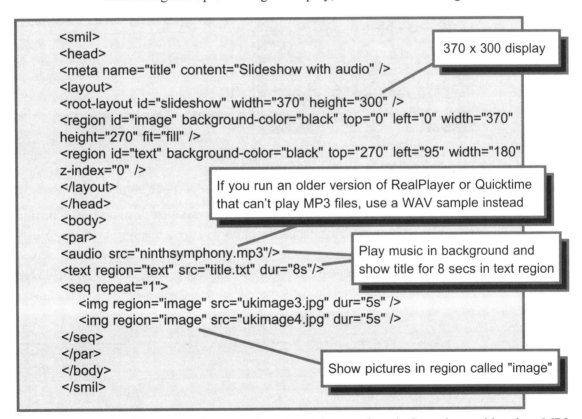

```
<smil>
<head>
<meta name="title" content="Slideshow with audio" />
<layout>
<root-layout id="slideshow" width="370" height="300" />
<region id="image" background-color="black" top="0" left="0" width="370"
height="270" fit="fill" />
<region id="text" background-color="black" top="270" left="95" width="180"
z-index="0" />
</layout>
</head>
<body>
<par>
<audio src="ninthsymphony.mp3"/>
<text region="text" src="title.txt" dur="8s"/>
<seq repeat="1">
   <img region="image" src="ukimage3.jpg" dur="5s" />
   <img region="image" src="ukimage4.jpg" dur="5s" />
</seq>
</par>
</body>
</smil>
```

370 x 300 display

If you run an older version of RealPlayer or Quicktime that can't play MP3 files, use a WAV sample instead

Play music in background and show title for 8 secs in text region

Show pictures in region called "image"

For this page we have used our JPEG images from before, along with a short MP3 snippet of Beethoven's Ninth Symphony. The media type you won't have seen before – text – is simply a short message saved in .TXT format. As with all of the media links in this chapter, use whatever pictures or music files you like.

Along with **width** and **height**, several more region attributes are of importance. Setting its background colour is done by specifying either a colour name or a hexadecimal value. The **fit** attribute exists to tell the browser how an image should be displayed if the picture (or video) is a different size to the region. The options include *fill* (which stretches the picture to fill the region – which we have used) or *hidden* (the default – media is pushed up to the top-left hand corner of the region).

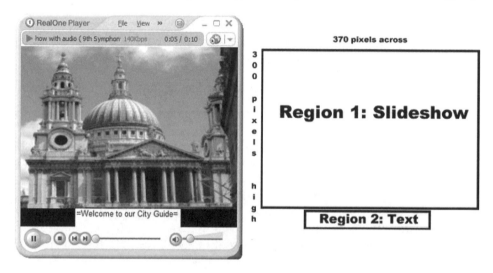

How the slideshow looks in RealOne Player alongside Region Map

Regions can overlap each other – for example a video displayed on a picture background. If you have overlapping regions you can add a final attribute to each region identifier. Z-index sets the z-order – that is, the order shapes are displayed when they overlap on a plane. We used z-index once in the code example – zero is the default setting. Every time you add a layer to a presentation give it a higher z-index (assuming it is to be displayed on top).

Tip

RealPlayer accommodates numerous extensions to SMIL, including RealText, for providing captioning and scrolling marquees. Consult the Real Networks documentation for more details: http://www.realnetworks.com/resources/

Embedding a presentation

Imagine you've written a SMIL presentation and it looks excellent. The difficulty now is that you want it to appear inside your web browser – perhaps as an audiovisual introduction to your site. You could try and get the SMIL to run inside the browser itself – which varies in difficulty because of differing standards – or embed the file as a RealPlayer object. The RealPlayer browser plug-in will work on Internet Explorer and the Netscape family of browsers (including open-source variants such as Mozilla).

Incorporating a presentation needs a few lines of code as this XHTML demo shows:

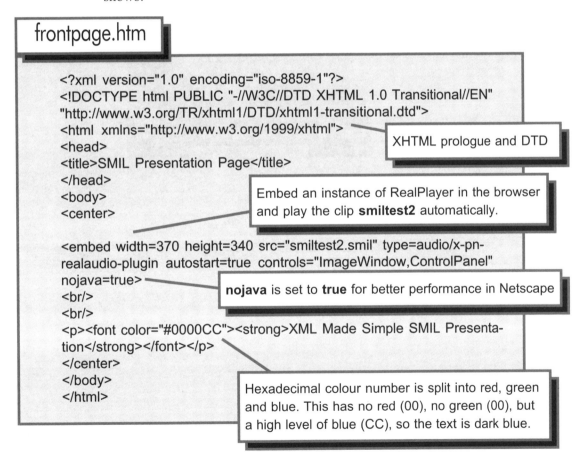

frontpage.htm

```
<?xml version="1.0" encoding="iso-8859-1"?>
<!DOCTYPE html PUBLIC "-//W3C//DTD XHTML 1.0 Transitional//EN"
"http://www.w3.org/TR/xhtml1/DTD/xhtml1-transitional.dtd">
<html xmlns="http://www.w3.org/1999/xhtml">
<head>
<title>SMIL Presentation Page</title>
</head>
<body>
<center>

<embed width=370 height=340 src="smiltest2.smil" type=audio/x-pn-
realaudio-plugin autostart=true controls="ImageWindow,ControlPanel"
nojava=true>
<br/>
<br/>
<p><font color="#0000CC"><strong>XML Made Simple SMIL Presenta-
tion</strong></font></p>
</center>
</body>
</html>
```

XHTML prologue and DTD

Embed an instance of RealPlayer in the browser and play the clip **smiltest2** automatically.

nojava is set to **true** for better performance in Netscape

Hexadecimal colour number is split into red, green and blue. This has no red (00), no green (00), but a high level of blue (CC), so the text is dark blue.

The EMBED tag has a list of attributes. RealPlayer is the default SMIL engine on this particular computer, so we give the type of data, the name of the file, whether to start as soon as the clip loads (**autostart=true**), and with the **controls** attribute, how to display the actual presentation window and what controls to include. We make the player window slightly bigger than the presentation window (340 pixels high instead of 300) so the start/stop controls do not lay across the text region.

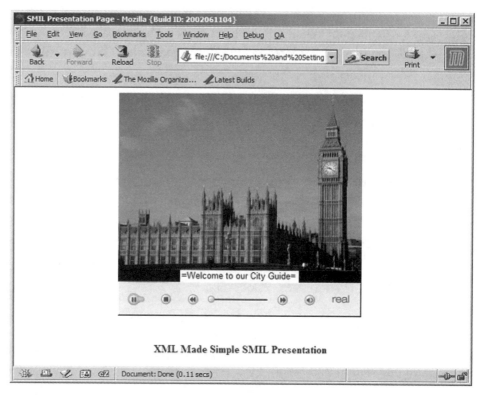

The presentation viewed in Mozilla

Popularising your site using XML

Weblogs and home pages

One of the problems faced by web designers is how to make people visit their pages. You can create the best-looking web site ever, but how do visitors know it has been updated? What if you've added lots of interesting new content, but hardly anybody bothers to check? In an ideal world you would be able to send out snippets of information telling users about updated content. Theoretically an e-mail mailing list does this – but only to people who have registered their details. Your site may show up on search engines, but not high enough up the list for many people to discover it.

Recently there has been an enormous rise in what are called weblogs. A weblog is effectively an online journal and contains a series of dated entries. Weblogs tend to be non-commercial and are filled with general musings on an endless variety of subjects. With free software (e.g. Blogger: http://www.blogger.com/about.pyra) anybody can set up a weblog, and these are rapidly becoming the modern equivalent of personal home pages. Many professionals are now getting their own blog pages, which gives them an easy way to speak about important issues of the day. The blogging concept has been further extended to allow users to post comments (much like the USENET news system), and complex discussions ensue.

A blog is the sort of page that is likely to change at unpredictable intervals. A near-automatic system of advertising the blog would have links that change along with the site, together with data about the changed content. This system would be versatile enough to handle any web site that wishes to syndicate data. Web developers are currently excited over an XML-based family of content description languages, known by the generic term '*RSS*'.

Take note

The term 'web-log' is often shortened to 'blog', and is also used as a verb. People who write weblogs are therefore known as 'bloggers'.

Rich Site Summary

Rich Site Summary (RSS) format is based on XML and allows the creation of content 'feeds', consisting of hyperlinks and metadata. A web site will have a list of content it wishes to make available. A URL links to an RSS file on the site, describing this data. RSS links usually have an identifying ▆RSS▆ ▆XML▆ logo.

There are a number of news reader applications that support the RSS format. The way these work is that a user will come across a web site they like and they then add the URL for its RSS feed into their reader. This program runs in the background on their client machine and periodically monitors the feed. When the feed changes, the reader alerts the user. Most web surfers have a small group of sites they check up on regularly, and their favourite site's RSS feeds are loaded into the reader. In this way the user is notified when material changes and is free to browse through a précis of the new content without having to spend time on the site looking through pages of text. The user might also wish to download news for later reading offline, especially those who connect to the Internet via a dial-up link.

Windows users can download a freeware news reader program called Feedreader, from http://www.feedreader.com. If you have a different operating system, try the Hotsheet program from: http://www.johnmunsch.com/projects/HotSheet. This reader is written in Java and should work on almost any platform.

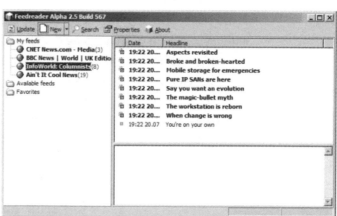

Take note

There are many versions of RSS. This is also the case with the acronym. RSS is also used to mean 'RDF Site Summary' or 'Really Simple Syndication'.

The Feedreader program running technology, general and movie news feeds

Aggregators

News reader programs come with categorised links that help get you started. Web portals have emerged whose main function is to act as aggregators of RSS data . Hence you can visit a site such as Meerkat (http://www.oreillynet.com/meerkat) and find news and information from hundreds of sources. Stories are split into categories (also called *channels*) – clicking on one results in you being taken to the material on the original source site. Therefore, allowing a content aggregator to use your RSS feed does not involve giving away content at all, the RSS data can be thought of as a publicity teaser. It is up to you how much content you wish to place in the RSS feed. There are aggregators for all manner of information – even weblogs. Bloggers can submit their RSS feed to an aggregator (which may itself be a popular blog site, like Blogger.com) and reach a much wider audience than they otherwise would.

RSS can help give you dynamic content on your web site. For instance many small web companies now use free news feeds (RSS-based) to place headlines on their front page. This encourages users to visit the site as they know that new material will automatically be posted when it becomes available. The companies that produce the feeds will provide a moderated list of stories from many sources, thus saving the small site designer the job of manually checking through feeds to find the most interesting stories.

Businesses providing these services make money by providing premium content for commercial web sites, although a few offer basic RSS services gratis. One such site is News is Free (http://www.newsisfree.com/syndicate.php) who have a headline service for non-profit users.

RSS standards

What does an RSS feed actually look like? There are around half a dozen slightly different formats. The original version (0.9) was designed by Netscape and looks similar to an earlier attempt to syndicate data with XML, CDF (Channel Definition Format), version 0.91 soon followed, promoted by Userland Software.

A RSS page will consist of a channel definition (i.e. metadata about your site) as a root element, with one or more items (the hyperlinks and headlines) inside it.

Version 1.0 of RSS is based around a existing XML standard for metadata – the Resource Description Framework (RDF), and makes use of XML namespaces. RDF is a standard for transferring metadata, not a list of specific metadata tags. Users of RDF can create their own schemas for particular uses, for example the Dublin Core Module. This was formulated by information specialists to provide an easier way of exchanging metadata – RSS 1.0 uses Dublin Core. A 1.0 file actually has a different channel/item structure. Instead of everything being held inside the channel tags, the channel data is defined first, followed by an item list.

The latest version of RSS, 2.0 is a little simpler, and at first sight appears almost identical to RSS 0.91. The three versions of RSS we have mentioned so far are all co-existing with each other, although it is expected that versions 0.9x will become obsolete soon. News reader programs try to be compatible with each of the main RSS standards, but some web sites either use an obscure RSS standard or do not adhere correctly to the XML rules on making their content well-formed, making their feeds unusable.

The next example, feed.rss, is a small illustration of a version 2.0 RSS feed.

As you can see from this, it is fairly easy to create your own basic RSS files in a text editor. Making RSS feeds automatically is done by a process called **scraping**. A scraping program scans a web site and attempts to find relevant items for syndication. Scraping can be a complex business depending on the nature of your site – many programmers build database-backed systems that generate pages dynamically and they can alter their code to output a RSS feed automatically. If you use content management software to maintain a large site, check to see if it has an option for outputting RSS feeds. For beginners or the curious, a few online tools exist which make RSS feeds from web sites. If you have a home page and wish to experiment, go to **MyRSS** (http://myrss.com) and see what kind of feed is automatically generated from your site.

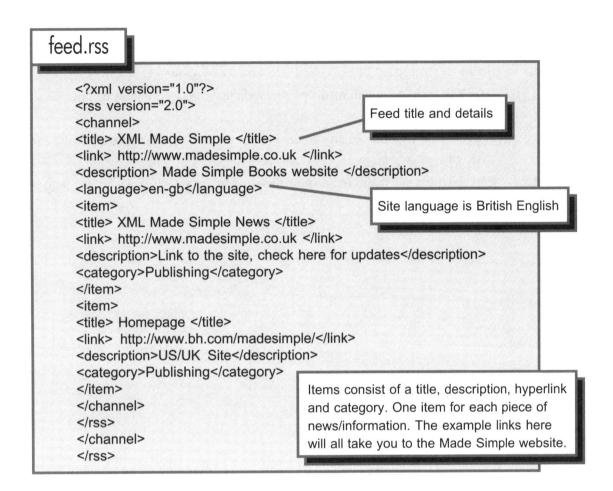

feed.rss

```
<?xml version="1.0"?>
<rss version="2.0">
<channel>
<title> XML Made Simple </title>
<link> http://www.madesimple.co.uk </link>
<description> Made Simple Books website </description>
<language>en-gb</language>
<item>
<title> XML Made Simple News </title>
<link> http://www.madesimple.co.uk </link>
<description>Link to the site, check here for updates</description>
<category>Publishing</category>
</item>
<item>
<title> Homepage </title>
<link> http://www.bh.com/madesimple/</link>
<description>US/UK Site</description>
<category>Publishing</category>
</item>
</channel>
</rss>
</channel>
</rss>
```

Feed title and details

Site language is British English

Items consist of a title, description, hyperlink and category. One item for each piece of news/information. The example links here will all take you to the Made Simple website.

Take note

There is currently work in progress towards creating new XML news languages, for facilitating data interchange between the big media corporations. Among these are NewsML and the News Industry Text Format (http://iptc.org/).

Exercises

1   Create a SMIL page that plays a video over a background image.

2   Use SMIL to make a multimedia presentation featuring a slideshow on one side of the display and a video on the other.

3   Create a RSS feed for our city guide. For the purposes of illustration, call the site URL city-test-site.com.

4   Can you think of a major reason why people would want to use RSS rather than e-mail notifiers?

9 WAP and mobile devices

Mobiles and the Internet

Several years ago mobile phone companies began to release products which could access the Internet. A mobile phone has a number of shortcomings that make this a difficult task – the device has limited memory, works on batteries and a screen that only allows a few lines of text to be displayed at once. Clearly a conventional web page will not display on a tiny monochrome screen so engineers set out to produce software systems that allow for viewing of simplified Internet sites.

In Japan the I-mode standard used a cut-down version of HTML. European engineers however opted for a slightly different route and created a new XML-based language called WML. *Wireless Markup Language* is built into the micro-browsers (often called *user-agents*) on mobiles. These devices use a suite of networking applications known as the *Wireless Application Protocol* (WAP), which have been built from scratch to allow efficient transportation of small amounts of data across the Internet. Most mobiles still use the GSM (Global System for Mobile communications) standard so transfer rates are very slow. Data rates are measured in bits per second (bps) – a GSM phone works at 9600 bps as compared to a conventional computer modem rate of 56000 bps – though these numbers are a theoretical maxim rather than the average rate. As one byte is equal to eight bits, a GSM connection can receive around 1Kb (1024 bytes) of data per second.

Take note

The I-Mode language is called CWML (Compact Wireless Markup Language), not to be confused with WML on WAP phones. The USA does not use GSM, but a competing standard called CDMA (Code-Division Multiple Access).

WAP technology

A collection of web pages mixed with server-based programs is generally referred to as a web application. The same terminology is used for WAP, but traditional web pages are not a part of WAP. Instead of having HTML files which might be 20 or 30 kilobytes in size, WAP opts for storing a series of mini-pages – called *cards* – in a single file. A series of cards make up a *deck* – analogous to a web site. This makes perfect sense because it allows the phone to load several pages at once, thus reducing the time it takes to fetch data from the network.

No special technology is needed by the WAP programmer for hosting his or her pages. Sites aimed at mobile users are stored on regular web servers, running HTTP. The clever technology lies in the WAP gateways that convert the data into a format usable on the mobile devices. Typically a gateway will be owned by the phone company or a large business and your mobile will be set to communicate with it. All the mobile user has to do is type in the address of the pages required and the gateway will oversee the process of fetching them. The gateway will translate HTTP data into a more compact final form, using a process called *compilation*.

With computer programs, compiling involves turning the text of the source file into a lower-level machine code the computer understands. Compiling WAP pages is more a matter of *tokenising* them to reduce space than turning them into machine code. Tokenisation takes a series of often used words and converts them into a brief numerical code (token). With WML we know that a few dozen words are used all the time, so by compressing these the overall size of a deck is reduced. Newer mobile systems have quite large memories, but to retain compatibility with the earlier ones a deck size of about 1400 bytes of tokenised data is the approximate upper limit. This amounts to several pages of code and you can split a WAP site up into several decks. As with XML, excess white space between elements is ignored and the parser sets all spaces to a single character unless told otherwise.

Tip

WML has special characters very similar to those in XML. An extra space can be added by including the ** ** entity. A left angle bracket with **&lt**, a right one with **&gt** and so on.

Testing WAP pages

If you want to create and view mobile pages you have several options. You can set up a web server on your own PC, and configure it to host WAP data. While the configuration process involves making the server recognise the new file types (by altering what are called the MIME options), it is not recommended if you are just learning about WAP. Alternatively, you can purchase web space via a hosting company, who will be able to deal with any configuration issues arising.

Viewing WAP sites is normally done via your mobile phone or PDA, however this option is unlikely to be free and you may end up with a large phone bill. Developers tend to get around the need for a real mobile by using an *emulator* program. This is an application you install on your PC that duplicates the functionality of another computer – in this case a WAP device. There are many WAP emulators on the Web ranging from Java-based pop-up programs to downloadable emulators designed to simulate the functions of a particular phone. Emulators generally will load pages that exist on the Internet, so are good if you are hosting your pages on a remote machine, or using a web server.

To see your WAP pages on an emulator, enter the URL as you would with a conventional web site. The addresses for WAP sites tend to be slightly shorter than their WWW equivalents because of the difficulty of typing out long strings of letters on a mobile keypad.

Take note

If you are unable or unwilling (perhaps for security reasons) to use your own web server, there are applications which act as plain **WAP** browsers and allow you to load **WML** files straight from a directory.

Take note

If your pages are running on your own personal server, then you should be able to load them into an emulator by entering the generic local machine address (it is always the same for your computer to access internally – external machines will call your proper IP address):

127.0.0.1

WAP browsers

A WAP browser program is any Internet browser that will correctly display WML files. Of the three most widely established web browsing applications, only Opera will allow you to load surf WAP sites by default. Opera is a good choice because versions are available for the Macintosh and Linux platforms.

If you do not wish to install a full-scale application like Opera, there are several mini-browsers available on the PC specially geared for mobile pages. The browser you will see in some of the example screenshots is called WinWap.

The procedure for creating our WML pages is almost identical to our previous XML projects:

1   Create your files in a text editor (we have used Notepad but any similar application, like BBEdit on the Macintosh will do).

2   Save the files with the extension .**WML**. In the examples here we have saved all the files into a folder called waptest on the C: drive.

3   To test your pages in WinWap, go to **File**, then **Open Location**, browse to *C:/ waptest/* and load the relevant page.

4   To test your pages in Opera, go to **File**, then **Open**. You will be presented with a window, click in the **File of Type** drop-down list and select *All files*. Your test pages will now appear when you go to *C:/waptest/*

In the remainder of this chapter we will have a crash course on how to make your own WML decks. We do not cover the WMLscripting language (the aim is to look at the XML-like elements of WML), but you may be surprised at the number of things you can do with plain WML pages.

> ## Tip
>
> You can download a trial version of WinWap from the Winwap.org site at: http://www.winwap.org/winwap/download.html
>
> It will install on Windows 95 version and above.

A WML page

Let's create a WML page. Type in this code and load it into your WAP browser.

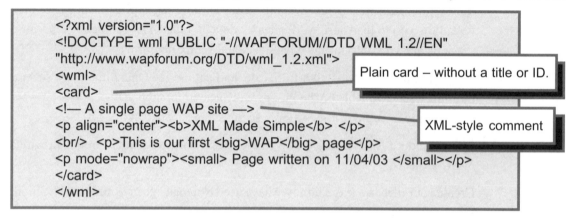

```
<?xml version="1.0"?>
<!DOCTYPE wml PUBLIC "-//WAPFORUM//DTD WML 1.2//EN"
"http://www.wapforum.org/DTD/wml_1.2.xml">
<wml>
<card>
<!— A single page WAP site —>
<p align="center"><b>XML Made Simple</b> </p>
<br/>  <p>This is our first <big>WAP</big> page</p>
<p mode="nowrap"><small> Page written on 11/04/03 </small></p>
</card>
</wml>
```

Plain card – without a title or ID.

XML-style comment

Unsurprisingly, this code bears a strong resemblance to other XML languages, with a few slight differences. The root element **<wml>** defines a deck. Inside this are one or more cards. Here we have a single card containing three paragraphs (defined with the **<p>** tag). The first is centred and in bold. It is followed by a line break and a paragraph set to the (default) left alignment. A final paragraph displays the date in small font, with the mode set to 'wrap' so that any incomplete word at the end of the screen is carried to the next line. If the mode is set to 'nowrap', words will continue off-screen and the user will need to scroll horizontally to see them.

Usability and visual consistency between browsers is a major topic among web developers. The WAP standard is designed for devices with small monochrome screens, with simple text formatting capabilities. Even then you cannot be certain how a page will look. Here is our first page in Opera and WinWap – Opera doesn't like to centre the title text, and includes wider spacing than WinWap.

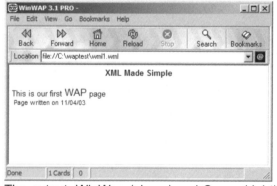

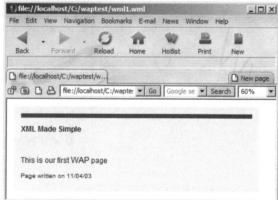

The output: WinWap (above) and Opera (right)

Multiple cards

To produce a workable WAP site we require a method of navigating from one page to another. Under HTML a page can link to an outside file, or to an identifier within itself (an anchor). WML uses the same concept to allow easy navigation between cards. Creating links couldn't be easier – give each of your cards an **id** attribute, and use a hyperlink **<a href>** tag to connect between them. The code below has both examples with navigation between cards and several links to external sites.

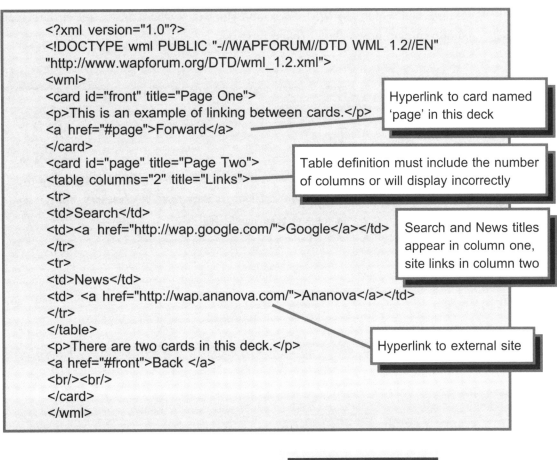

```
<?xml version="1.0"?>
<!DOCTYPE wml PUBLIC "-//WAPFORUM//DTD WML 1.2//EN"
"http://www.wapforum.org/DTD/wml_1.2.xml">
<wml>
<card id="front" title="Page One">
<p>This is an example of linking between cards.</p>
<a href="#page">Forward</a>
</card>
<card id="page" title="Page Two">
<table columns="2" title="Links">
<tr>
<td>Search</td>
<td><a href="http://wap.google.com/">Google</a></td>
</tr>
<tr>
<td>News</td>
<td> <a href="http://wap.ananova.com/">Ananova</a></td>
</tr>
</table>
<p>There are two cards in this deck.</p>
<a href="#front">Back </a>
<br/><br/>
</card>
</wml>
```

Hyperlink to card named 'page' in this deck

Table definition must include the number of columns or will display incorrectly

Search and News titles appear in column one, site links in column two

Hyperlink to external site

Screenshot of program two on Opera

Page Two

Search Google
News   Ananova

There are two cards in this deck.

Back

In the second card we have created a table, very much like those in HTML pages. A table consists of a number of columns, each defined with **<td>** elements. Whatever is held between these elements is displayed in a single cell of the table. A new row is created by using the **<tr>** element. We use tables to make sure data displays in a tidy way. Before style sheets came to be used on HTML pages, tables were the only way to be certain that text would be formatted correctly in fields (e.g. a line listing name, age and phone number would have three fields corresponding to three table columns). WML uses tables for exactly the same reason, as the screen shot of program two shows (page 113).

Tip

To jump between cards, you can also use the <anchor> element. For example <anchor>Go Back<prev/> </anchor> will return to the last page you visited.

Mobile-compatible images

Having pure text pages is of limited use – in many cases similar information can be conveyed by text message for lesser cost. The mobile device should have the ability to show pictures, while taking into account the low memory and transmission speeds of most phones. The initial solution was to opt for monochrome images. The number of colours on a computer image is given by how many bits there are to each pixel. With 4 bits there are 16 combinations, and so 16 colours on screen, with 8 bits (a byte per pixel) there are 256 combinations. A monochrome screen can represent each pixel with a single bit – it is either on (black) or off (white). This means that a single byte can hold the values for 8 pixels. The resolution of mobile screens is typically very low (less than 10,000 pixels compared to a typical PC screen resolution of nearly a million), so a full-screen image is easily stored in a kilobyte or under.

WAP devices use the WBMP (Wireless BitMap) file format to hold image files. Normal image files have to be converted to the WBMP format which can involve a serious loss of definition. To create a WMBP image you will need a graphics program such as Paint Shop Pro or Adobe Photoshop. The newest version of Paint Shop Pro allows direct conversion to the WBMP format. However, if you own an earlier version, you should proceed as follows:

1 Create a new image and set the image type to 2 colours (1 bit).

2 Make sure the resolution of the picture isn't greater than that of your mobile's screen. A 100 × 80 pixel image would fit on most screens.

3 Draw your picture using black and white pixels and save it as *picname.BMP*.

4 The bitmap image now has to be converted to WBMP format. Fortunately there are several tools around to do this online. A good one is the TeraFlops converter based at: http://www.teraflops.com/wbmp/

5 Load your BMP picture into the converter and when prompted save the resulting WBMP file. If you want to convert a picture rather than create one, you will have to resize (or use the resample option on PSP) the image and reduce its colour depth to two colours or the conversion process will fail.

Converting between image formats is a tricky business and results are not always good. If you wish to convert more than a few pictures to WBMP format it may be worth using a program such as ImageMagick (http://www.imagemagick.org/), which is available for most platforms, including the Macintosh.

Inserting the image

Incorporating your new image into a WML page could not be easier, and once again is effectively identical to HTML. We use an **<img>** tag containing the name of the image file:

```
<?xml version="1.0"?>
<!DOCTYPE wml PUBLIC "-//WAPFORUM//DTD WML 1.2//EN"
"http://www.wapforum.org/DTD/wml_1.2.xml">
<wml>
<card id="front" title="Welcome">
<p align="center">                    Image is centred
<img src="logo.wbmp"  alt="Front page"/>
</p>
</card>
</wml>
```

For this page we made a small logo (100 × 100 pixels – a real phone logo would be slightly smaller) for our city guide page, and converted it using the Teraflops converter. You will see that after the filename, there is an **alt** attribute – this contains a brief text string that will be shown if the mobile device for some reason cannot display the image (as with HTML pages).

Logo shown in WinWap browser

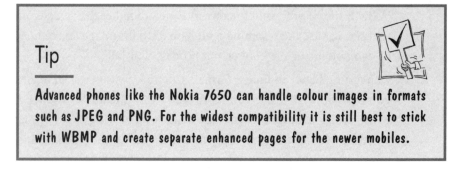

Tip

Advanced phones like the Nokia 7650 can handle colour images in formats such as JPEG and PNG. For the widest compatibility it is still best to stick with WBMP and create separate enhanced pages for the newer mobiles.

Input, events and timers

The utility of WML is extended by the use of events. An event is when an action is triggered that causes the computer to do something. The designers of WML have opted to include simple event handling as part of the markup language itself, along with rudimentary variable handling capabilities.

In WML there are several events triggered either by the user (you press a button) or the browser (a timer executes). The default WML timer counts down in 1/10 second decrements. To use a timer we have to tell the browser how long the timer should run, and what it should do when the countdown is complete. A typical use of timers is to produce splash screens or advertisements that stay on view for a few seconds. The next program introduces this and several other things that we haven't seen up to now in our outline of WML coding.

The first card contains a text advertising message that shows on the browser for 4 seconds (40 × 1/10) before redirecting to a card which requires user input. A drop-down list asks for the user to choose a city and then click on the hyperlink. The value of the drop-down box is actually a WML variable, and its state (value) is held within the deck. To print a variable on screen, the name is enclosed in parentheses and prefixed by a dollar sign (a little like the scripting language PERL):

```
<p> The variable result is: $(variable) </p>
```

Variables in WML can either be set by user input, or during a task (called when an event occurs). A timer hitting zero is one event, others include a link being selected, a button being pressed on the mobile, or the display being refreshed. In the listing we can see several tasks – the **<go>** task that jumps to the result card and the **<prev/>** task that jumps back a page. The final card refreshes the display and prints out the contents of the city variable – which should be identical to the city selected on the vote screen.

<setvar...>

Another way to set a variable's value is by using the **<setvar>** tag. Its syntax is:

```
<setvar name="variablename" value="variablevalue"/>
```

This allows the creation of new variables within a card. The rules on placing setvar are quite strict – and it must be placed between a **<refresh>**, **<go>** or **<prev>** element or else an error will result.

vote.wml

```
<?xml version="1.0"?>
<!DOCTYPE wml PUBLIC "-//WAPFORUM//DTD WML 1.2//EN"
"http://www.wapforum.org/DTD/wml_1.2.xml">
<wml>
<card id="sponsor" ontimer="#vote">
<timer value="40"/>
<p align="center">
And now a message from our sponsors.
</p>
<p align="center"><b>
<big> Made Simple Books are available at all good bookshops.</big>
</b></p>
<p align ="center"><small>
This is an advertising message
</small></p>
</card>
<card id="vote">
<p> Select your favourite city from<br/>
the drop-down list, then click on the link. </p>
<select name="city">
<option value="London"> London</option>
<option value="Birmingham"> Birmingham</option>
<option value="Edinburgh"> Edinburgh</option>
<option value="Liverpool"> Liverpool</option>
<option value="Manchester"> Manchester</option>
</select>
<p>
<anchor>
<go href="#result"/>
Result
</anchor>
</p>
</card>
<card id="result">
<p> You voted for: </p>
<p><b> $(city) </b></p>
<br/>
<anchor>Go Back<prev/> </anchor>
</card>
</wml>
```

Timer triggers after four seconds and sends browser to the vote card

Advertising screen

Select box set up with the name 'city' – its value depends on the option picked

User selection printed here

Illustrations showing the city selection deck on WinWap

Another tag of note is **<do>** which is also used to call a task. A common use of **<do>** is for push-button input on a mobile. A typical WAP phone will have two buttons underneath the screen that are used as shortcuts for yes/no, forward/back, etc. We can use **<do>** to facilitate the use of these buttons, by specifying the tag along with a suitable type parameter. Of these **Accept** (effectively an **OK** command) is used after some data has been input into a page, and prev to jump back a page. The following code should be very familiar based on what you've seen before:

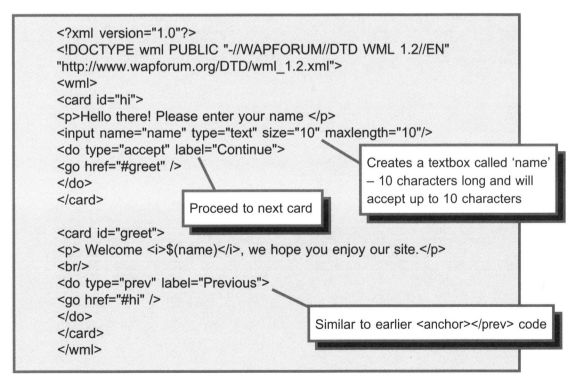

```
<?xml version="1.0"?>
<!DOCTYPE wml PUBLIC "-//WAPFORUM//DTD WML 1.2//EN"
"http://www.wapforum.org/DTD/wml_1.2.xml">
<wml>
<card id="hi">
<p>Hello there! Please enter your name </p>
<input name="name" type="text" size="10" maxlength="10"/>
<do type="accept" label="Continue">
<go href="#greet" />
</do>
</card>

<card id="greet">
<p> Welcome <i>$(name)</i>, we hope you enjoy our site.</p>
<br/>
<do type="prev" label="Previous">
<go href="#hi" />
</do>
</card>
</wml>
```

Creates a textbox called 'name' – 10 characters long and will accept up to 10 characters

Proceed to next card

Similar to earlier <anchor></prev> code

119

An input box is used to input your name. When the **Continue** button is pushed, the browser jumps to the second card, displays the name and uses a second **<do>** tag to let you go back a page.

<onevent>

The **<onevent>** tag is used to call an event with the syntax:

```
<onevent type="typeofevent">
<do some code>
</onevent>
```

The type attribute can be set to **onenterforward** (when we first come onto a page), **onentertbackward** (when we go back to a page), **onpick** (when an option is selected) and **ontimer**. We have not used **<onevent>** in this chapter because it produces unpredictable results on the test browsers, although its use is widespread in real-world WAP sites.

The future

In this chapter we have learnt the building-blocks of producing Internet pages for a mobile phone. WAP is still in its first incarnation. Phones now on the market feature colour screens, higher-resolution graphics, enough memory to run downloaded application software written in Java and much faster data transfer. GSM can be seen as the first generation mobile standard, the second is GPRS (General Packet Radio Switching) and allows for modem-level downloading speeds. You will have come across advertisements for 3G (Third Generation) phones – these offer even faster download speeds than GPRS and are poised to become the standard for mobile technology in the next decade.

Eventually WML will be too limiting to do what people require of a mobile Internet access device, but for the foreseeable future all Internet-ready phones will be compatible with the kinds of code we have written here today. Even when Europe and the USA switch to a new generation of phones, the number of people in other parts of the world owning version 1 WAP devices will still be in the hundreds of millions, so it makes sense to be able to cater for as wide an audience as possible. Fortunately, the newest version of the WAP protocol, WAP 2 incorporates support for a language to replace WML. That language is a version of XHTML with which you are already familiar.

Exercises

1   Create a simple animation using several cards and a timer event.

2   WML uses a tokenisation process to reduce the size of decks. With the help of variables, write some example code that performs basic text compression.

3   Create an example WML page for our city guide taking into account the limitations of mobile devices.

10 Real-world XML

XML tools

Once you have learnt the basics of XML you may wish to look for software that can enhance your coding skills and help you make better quality XML code. There are many XML tools on the market, and this section looks at a few of the most popular.

XMLSpy

XMLSpy is perhaps the most powerful commercial XML development environment available. It comes in three versions – Home (for students and occasional user), Professional and Enterprise (with advanced features such as web services facilities). You can download a 30 day trial version from http://www.altova.com/download.html. Altova also produce other useful XML tools such as **Stylevision** a XML web migration application and **Authentic** an XML document editor. XMLSpy is Windows only, but the latest version will work on Linux or MacOS running a suitable emulator, such as Wine (www.winehq.org/) or VirtualPC (see: www.microsoft.com/mac/products/virtualpc/virtualpc.aspx?pid=virtualpc). Users of the program will discover it has excellent document validation functions and a quantity of useful XML tools such as the DTD-Schema converter.

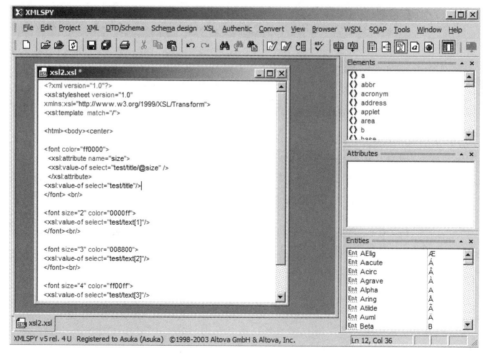

XMLSPY Enterprise Edition

Dreamweaver MX

This is an all-purpose commercial web development package with an XML-friendly editor that can handle Cascading Style Sheets and XHTML, and can convert from HTML to XHTML. You can download a free trial version for the Macintosh or PC from: http://www.macromedia.com/software/dreamweaver/.

Xerlin

Xerlin (http://www.xerlin.org/) is an open-source XML editor for Unix and Windows machines that uses the Java 2 platform, so you must have Java 2 installed on your computer. It presents a panel showing the XML elements, allowing you to add XML data or change attribute values in a document without directly altering the code. You can reuse elements and build up your own library of code templates.

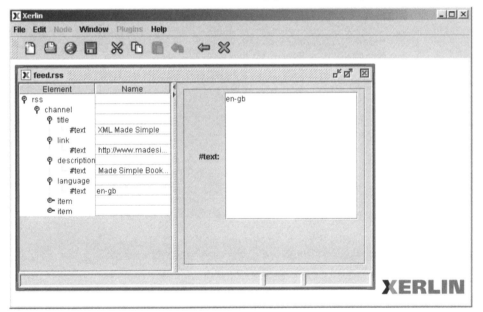

Xerlin Editor

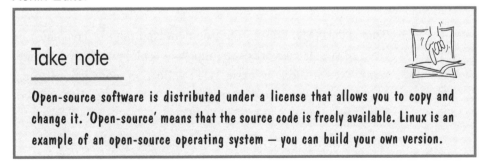

Take note

Open-source software is distributed under a license that allows you to copy and change it. 'Open-source' means that the source code is freely available. Linux is an example of an open-source operating system — you can build your own version.

jEdit

This is a powerful and attractive general-purpose text editor. jEdit is open-source and versions for Unix, Mac, OS/2 , Windows and VMS platforms are available from http://www.jedit.org/ – your computer will require a Java virtual machine for jEdit to work. Although jEdit is not XML specific, you can download some browser plug-ins that provide XML-related functions such as document validation.

Cooktop

Cooktop (http://www.xmlcooktop.com/) is a free XML editor for Windows. It has a number of useful features such as code tidying (removing excess spaces and other junk) and formatting, XPath debugging, XSL processing and XML validation.

Cooktop showing a document with an internal DTD

Xeena

This is the XML Editing Environment Naturally in Java and can be downloaded from IBM's Alphaworks site (http://www.alphaworks.ibm.com/tech/xeena). Currently Xeena supports basic DTD validation, connections to external (Internet-based) documents and XSL processing. The application will work on Windows, Unix and various flavours of MacOS.

126

SVG

You can write an XML document using a text editor or helper program, though XML application tend to be produced more often by software than by a programmer's labours. An example might be a drawing produced using a graphics program. A complex diagram could be hand-coded in SVG but normally graphics designers would create it with a program like Adobe Illustrator, which automatically converts the image into SVG.

SVG, the Scalable Vector Graphics system, is an XML application for describing 2D images. In a bitmap system, images are stored as a matrix of pixel colour values, whereas a vector application defines images as a series of commands and co-ordinates (draw a line here, draw a square there). The advantages of vector graphics are that they can be scaled (i.e. if you can redraw them on a higher resolution screen without stretching or image corruption) and file sizes tend to be much more compact than with bitmaps. SVG has complex facilities for text manipulation and vector animation.

SVG code has a number of similarities to SMIL, and allows the inclusion of CSS commands to format content. The rudimentary SVG program here draws three rectangles, each 400 pixels across by 100 pixels down, and adds some text.

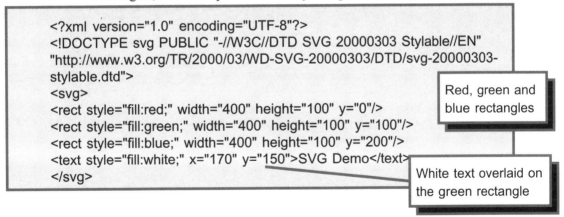

```
<?xml version="1.0" encoding="UTF-8"?>
<!DOCTYPE svg PUBLIC "-//W3C//DTD SVG 20000303 Stylable//EN"
"http://www.w3.org/TR/2000/03/WD-SVG-20000303/DTD/svg-20000303-
stylable.dtd">
<svg>
<rect style="fill:red;" width="400" height="100" y="0"/>
<rect style="fill:green;" width="400" height="100" y="100"/>
<rect style="fill:blue;" width="400" height="100" y="200"/>
<text style="fill:white;" x="170" y="150">SVG Demo</text>
</svg>
```

Red, green and blue rectangles

White text overlaid on the green rectangle

Take note

The next few XML applications are ones you might meet if you use graphics software, write scientific papers or use XML for e-business.

At present Macromedia's Flash is the most widespread vector graphics-based system, but SVG is gaining ground in several areas. You do not need any expensive software to design SVG and its XML standard is more open than Flash's proprietary coding.

Tip

You can view SVG on your web browser with a suitable plug-in program. Windows and Macintosh users may download a SVG viewer from Adobe's site at: http://www.adobe.com/svg/viewer/install/main.html. Unsupported versions for Linux and Solaris can be obtained from: http://www.adobe.com/svg/viewer/install/old.html. More experienced users may like to try Batik, a SVG toolkit written in Java: hyperlink http://xml.apache.org/batik/.

MathML

If you have a background in engineering or physics, you will know how difficult it can be to represent mathematical formulae on web pages. Languages like TeX are used for producing typeset output, but for web users, showing scientific papers can be a nightmare. There are several solutions, ranging from storing the formulae as image files, to converting the document in another format such as PDF.

MathML is a neat solution. Technical symbols are represented as two types of elements. *Presentation elements* are used to encode the formula's symbols, and *content elements* are used to describe their meaning. It is an output language for equation editors and maths programs and is not meant to be used directly by authors – encoding the formulae in ML tags by hand would be an incredibly tedious job. MathML is still evolving, and is presently up to version 2.0. To view pages containing MathML elements you need a browser like Mozilla with basic support built-in, or a MathPlayer plug-in (Windows users can download it from Design Science at http://www.dessci.com/en/products/mathplayer/download.asp).

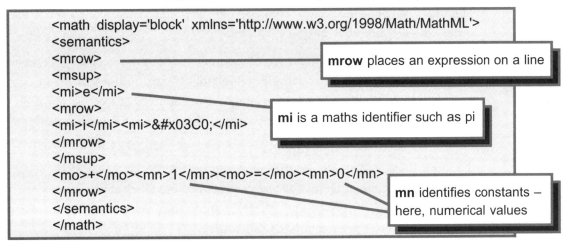

```
<math display='block' xmlns='http://www.w3.org/1998/Math/MathML'>
<semantics>
<mrow>
<msup>
<mi>e</mi>
<mrow>
<mi>i</mi><mi>&#x03C0;</mi>
</mrow>
</msup>
<mo>+</mo><mn>1</mn><mo>=</mo><mn>0</mn>
</mrow>
</semantics>
</math>
```

mrow places an expression on a line

mi is a maths identifier such as pi

mn identifies constants – here, numerical values

This displays the formula $e^{i\pi}+1=0$. MathML support is gaining ground and you should have some idea of it if you seek to do any kind of maths work on the Web.

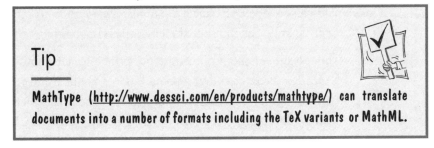

Tip

MathType (http://www.dessci.com/en/products/mathtype/) can translate documents into a number of formats including the TeX variants or MathML.

XML Encryption

Transferring data across computer networks causes massive security problems, especially if the data is XML documents because XML content can be read by any human. A variety of methods are used to make sure only authorised persons can see restricted data, the most important of which is encryption. An encryption system will take some data (the *plaintext*), perform mathematical transformations on it, and finish up with a resulting encoded (*ciphertext*) document that can only be understood by somebody with the correct password or electronic key.

A *symmetric* encryption system relies on a single key that is kept secret from everybody except those who own, or are authorised to decode the information. An *asymmetric* or '*public key*' system has a secret private key that is used to decode data, and a public key which anybody may use to send an encrypted file to the owner of the private key. By using what is called a *hash* code to check whether a file has been altered, together with symmetric encryption, programmers produce what are called '*digital signatures*'. If a file is digitally signed and the certificate correct then you can be sure that the file was created when the programmer said it was and that it has not been altered in any way by a third-party.

Encryption and digital signatures form the cornerstone of e-commerce systems and give a degree of trust to electronic transactions. With millions of credit card numbers, along with other private information (even medical records ultimately) travelling across public data channels, making this data secure from tampering is of the utmost importance.

The most-used system for securing data on the Internet is called **SSL** (Secure Sockets Layer), and provides a secure communications channel between computers. Much interest exists over a new XML security suite, based around applications called **XML Encryption** and **XML Signature**.

XML Encryption works by encoding elements in a document. Therefore while it can work like any other security software and encode whole files, XML Encryption also can encode only select elements. This ability to secure parts of a document right down to the individual element level is unique.

This document should illustrate the principle. Originally we would have a plain XML document containing some kind of medical information. The document is sent through XML Encryption software, which places encoded data between the **<cipherdata>** tags. Anybody reading the document would deduce the name of the person and that perhaps the document contained medical information, but could not find out anything else (in a real medical system all of the data would be encoded).

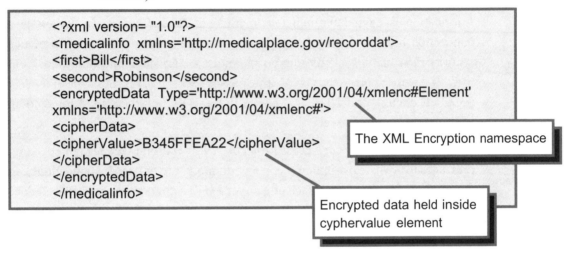

```
<?xml version= "1.0"?>
<medicalinfo xmlns='http://medicalplace.gov/recorddat'>
<first>Bill</first>
<second>Robinson</second>
<encryptedData Type='http://www.w3.org/2001/04/xmlenc#Element'
xmlns='http://www.w3.org/2001/04/xmlenc#'>
<cipherData>
<cipherValue>B345FFEA22</cipherValue>
</cipherData>
</encryptedData>
</medicalinfo>
```

The XML Encryption namespace

Encrypted data held inside cyphervalue element

Tip

If you see a web page starting HTTPS:// (secure HTTP), this is a site using SSL. You can also tell by the lock icon that appears in the Status bar of your browser.

SOAP

Communicating across the Internet can be a tricky business. The existing protocols for sending data are not always compatible with each other and may be prone to hacking by malevolent users.

Information is passed through the Internet via the use of *ports*. A port is a connection number that a certain protocol will pass data to. In order to reduce security risks many systems administrators use a firewall application to lock out most of the open ports – thus preventing possible security breaches. One of the few ports left open is port 80, this is bound to the HTTP protocol used for sending information across the web.

SOAP, the Simple Object Access Protocol, revolves around the idea of encoding messages in XML. Distributed (i.e. network, multi-server based) applications can then share information with each other over a HTTP connection. SOAP itself does not do anything other than specify a message framework. It is up to the end users to write software which interprets the SOAP messages. As SOAP uses XML it facilitates platform-independent data transfer.

To construct a SOAP message we set up the SOAP namespace and place the relevant XML code inside a **<body>** element. An optional header passes relevant data (e.g. the message number, expiry date or request or similar) to the server.

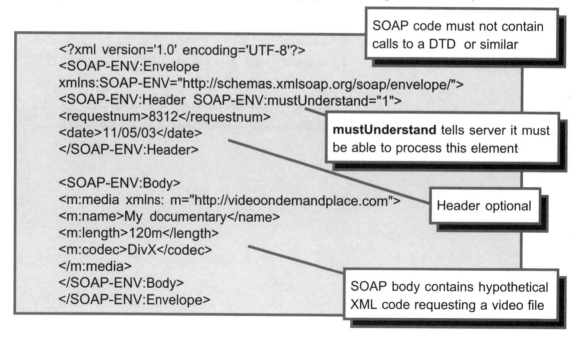

```
<?xml version='1.0' encoding='UTF-8'?>
<SOAP-ENV:Envelope
xmlns:SOAP-ENV="http://schemas.xmlsoap.org/soap/envelope/">
<SOAP-ENV:Header  SOAP-ENV:mustUnderstand="1">
<requestnum>8312</requestnum>
<date>11/05/03</date>
</SOAP-ENV:Header>

<SOAP-ENV:Body>
<m:media xmlns: m="http://videoondemandplace.com">
<m:name>My  documentary</name>
<m:length>120m</length>
<m:codec>DivX</codec>
</m:media>
</SOAP-ENV:Body>
</SOAP-ENV:Envelope>
```

SOAP code must not contain calls to a DTD or similar

mustUnderstand tells server it must be able to process this element

Header optional

SOAP body contains hypothetical XML code requesting a video file

A typical SOAP exchange between computers features a series of request/response messages. The client machine sends a SOAP request asking for some information, this is processed on the server and a response is returned with the results. Errors result in a fault message being returned, such as the following example.

```
<?xml version='1.0' encoding='UTF-8'?>
<SOAP-ENV:Envelope
xmlns:SOAP-ENV="http://schemas.xmlsoap.org/soap/envelope/">
<SOAP-ENV:Body>
<SOAP-ENV:Fault>
<faultcode> SOAP-ENV: MustUnderstand</faultcode>
<faultstring> Did not understand Header</faultstring>
</SOAP-ENV:Fault>
</SOAP-ENV:Body>
</SOAP-ENV:Envelope>
```

MustUnderstand Faultcode shows failure to understand a mustUnderstand element

Faultstring is a plain text description of the error

SOAP is expected to become the main protocol for exchanging XML information, and therefore will form a central pillar of the upcoming web services revolution.

Web services

You might have heard the term 'web services' mentioned in several contexts. In the XML world, a web service is an Internet application that makes extensive use of XML for communicating and processing data. Internet-based applications are written in a variety of languages and the majority are not designed to interact with any others. A web service can communicate and share data with other programs across the Internet. In the past this kind of software was expensive to create because the Internet runs on a multitude of incompatible platforms. Web services communicate via XML messaging using systems such as SOAP and WSDL (Web Services Description Language), thus removing this limitation.

WSDL file are XML documents that describe a web service in terms of message components. A WSDL document will therefore consist of a list of commands defining the messages, communications protocols and request types (i.e. a one way message, or a two way communication) used in a web service.

Companies, governments and other large organisations have taken to performing important data-processing operations online and web services will be an integral part of this strategy. Placing operations online allows institutions to take advantage of the latest technology and – in theory at least – save money by capitalising on the Internet's distributed nature. Imagine an electronic market site where the user sees a front end web page that lists prices from hundreds of different vendors. In the past this information might have to be entered manually by teams of people; programmers could write software to carry out the functions, but the lack of a single web communications architecture would make this an expensive proposition.

Using web services, the software running on the market server could converse with the computers on the vendor's sites using XML and request the pricing data automatically. Of course the vendors might give the information away for free (to perhaps enhance their commercial profile), or may sell it via some type of subscription system. Barriers to market entry are lowered because the web service

Tip

The Web Services Interoperability Organisation is devoted to formulating new web services standards and practices. Their site (http://ws-i.org) is well worth a visit.

standards should work across any platform and programming development systems often have web service support built-in.

An example of a web service is MS Passport, the log-in system used in Hotmail and Microsoft Messenger. Third parties can use Passport to provide authentication for their own web-sites. It works out cheaper for participating companies to rent their log-in services through Passport than to build an account security system from scratch.

A typical web service consists of software written in any Internet-applicable language (i.e. PERL, C++, ASP), but which obeys the standard messaging protocols. In one way you can think of web services as objects in a massive object-oriented network. Presently the two most widely used development systems for web services are Microsoft's .NET framework and Sun's Java platform. Java is a language specially designed for distributed computing and is the market leader at the moment. The .NET standard is still evolving, .NET applications can be written in several languages, including the new language C#.

The actual web service code is generally located on Internet servers, although smaller devices may run web-service-type applications and are known as 'smart clients' (e.g. a mobile phone that swapped documents directly with another phone).

Tip

Sun Microsystem's Java web services technology page is found at:
http://java.sun.com/webservices/

Further information on the .NET framework can be obtained from Microsoft's site:
http://www.microsoft.com/net/

Enhancing documents

We have touched upon the concept of metadata and how that can help improve searching and cataloguing of information. Making web pages easier to search through is not the only thing metadata can do. We saw earlier how you can enclose meta information in SMIL presentations and RSS feeds (some versions of RSS use a metadata format called Resource Description Framework). Similarly Schema annotations can help make data easier to process and give extra information to the systems using the schema.

This concept can be extended to files in general with powerful results. Imagine if a piece of software encodes metadata describing alterations to a document, or details about where a digital image was produced. Such information often exists but is in a hard to understand format, and so software companies are beginning to add XML-based metadata into their applications. Eventually many file formats will be replaced by XML documents – allowing anybody to swap files and information without the need for conversion programs – and XSL transformations will be used to render them on screen. However vendor-independent file systems could prove a commercial threat to established software companies (if a cheaper database system can process all your data in the same format just as efficiently, why pay for the expensive one?), so progress towards full integration and independence may be slow.

Take note

The latest Adobe applications such as GoLive! and Photoshop use metadata to enhance document files with the XMP (Extensible Metadata Platform) format: http://www.adobe.com/products/xmp/main.html.

The open source business suite Open Office (http://www.openoffice.org) has comprehensive XML-based file format support, including MathML for equation-laden documents. Microsoft's Office 2003 also comes with XML file capabilities (http://www.microsoft.com/office) as standard.

Looking forward

The next stage in the evolution of the Internet will be the *semantic Web* – a future World Wide Web built around XML and making heavy use of metadata to assign meaning to documents. Such documents would be processed by very advanced software applications called *agents*. The use of XML to attach meaning lets only the most pertinent information be picked – in theory this means no more situations where a specific search request would return ten million hits of dubious relevance.

A web browser is often called a user agent as it fulfils the criteria of reacting to a user's requests (e.g. when you select a page). The type of agents envisaged here would be semi-autonomous programs that need not be tied to a single computer and can travel around the Internet.

The agents would not be artificially intelligent in any significant way, but programmed with certain preferences and the capacity to independently react to a user's requests. Therefore searching databases or looking through web pages for a specific piece of information becomes far easier as millions of small programs do the job currently performed by massive centralised search engines and database management systems. If this vision becomes a reality, future generations of the Internet will be a lot more responsive, efficient and relevant to the user who may be accessing the networks using one of the many different types of web-enabled devices on the market. The downside will be how this information processing capacity and openness of data changes society and its effect on privacy, security and the global economic system.

Over the past ten chapters we have seen how to build XML documents and looked at some of the most popular XML technologies. In the coming years XML and related applications will become ubiquitous and a basic knowledge of XML essential for any Information Technology worker. We hope that the background material we have presented here will help you in your future XML activities.

Web sites

There are no formal exercises for this chapter. Instead, we propose you further investigate some of the technologies and systems described in the book and see how they may change the way we use computers in the near future. The W3C site (http://www.w3.org/) contains the most up to date XML documentation all available for free download. They have a section devoted to the concepts behind the Semantic Web: http://www.w3.org/2001/sw/.

If you have a background in programming and are interested in looking into the issues of web services in more detail, here are a few more sites of interest:

Web services for PERL programmers:

http://www.soaplite.com/

Apple WebObjects Web service guide:

http://www.apple.com/webobjects/web_services.html

For an example of web services in action, Amazon are allowing programmers to create sample XML applications that utilise the ecommerce giant's comprehensive product catalogue. Participation is free to interested parties:

http://www.amazon.com/gp/browse.html/104-8872776-4940725?node=3435361

For further information on .NET's Passport system, go to:

http://www.microsoft.com/net/services/passport/

Increasingly databases are supporting XML. The technology is still in flux as software producers attempt to find the best way of processing XML efficiently inside a database. Some sites of interest for those with database experience are:

Oracle's XML Technology Center:

http://otn.oracle.com/tech/xml/index.html

Microsoft SQL Server and XML:

http://www.microsoft.com/sql/techinfo/xml/default.asp

Appendices

XML overview

The typical XML document structure is:

```
<?xml version="1.0" encoding="ISO-8859-1" standalone="yes"?>
<!DOCTYPE mydoc SYSTEM "mydoc.dtd">
<root>
<!— comment —>
  <element1>
    <element2>
      <elementx>
        Some data
      </elementx>
    </element2>
  </element1>
</root>
```

All XML documents must include a declaration in the first line describing the language version. The declaration may also contain a reference to the character set using the **encoding** attribute. Typical values for European language users are "ISO-8859-1" or "UTF-8" – both being subsets of the Unicode character system. If the **standalone** attribute is included in the declaration, the document does not call any external documents and is self-contained. The declaration is part of the XML prologue containing **system processing directives** placed before the actual code. Also included in a possible prologue would be lines calling a document type definition (as shown) or referencing a stylesheet.

Following this is the root element that is the container for every other element. When an element is nested inside another one we say that the parent element contains one (or more) child elements.

Comments are ignored by the computer but provide information to programmers.

Element summary

An XML element consists of an open and close tag and the information it encloses.

```
<element> Element data </element>
```

If a tag does not contain any information, it must still be closed. A shorthand method is used where a single tag with closing symbol – this is an *empty element*:

```
<element></element>     Open and close.
<element />             Shorthand version (NB: space after element name).
```

An empty element can have a space after the name but not after the / symbol – <element />, not <element/ > or <element / >.

Elements are case-sensitive. The computer will treat the following as three entirely separate elements, rather than three instances of the same element:

```
<book/>       All lower-case.
<BOOK/>       All capitals.
<bOOk/>       Mixed-case.
```

Attributes pass values to elements. The values must be enclosed in quote marks. Single or double quotes are fine, as long as they match:

```
<name first="Lori" age='20'/>    Double and single quotes – works
<name first='Billy' age='25'/>   Single quotes only – works
<name first="Katie" age="22'/>   Age has mixed quotes – gives error
```

Attributes and names

Data can be stored in attributes, or in nested elements. This is decided by the rules laid down in the DTD. The information held in these two examples is equivalent:

```
<scientist name="Newton" work="gravity, calculus"/>    Uses attributes
<scientist>                                             Uses elements
<name>Newton</name>
<work>gravity</work>
<work>calculus</work>
</scientist>
```

There are a few limitations on element names. Elements cannot start with a number, contain spaces or any characters such as an ampersand, although you may space parts of an element with an underline character:

```
<el_a/>      Correct – contains underline
<7el_a/>     Error – starts with a number
<el&a/>      Error – contains forbidden character
<el a/>      Error – contains space
```

You may nest elements one within one another (all elements are nested inside the root), but an opening and closing tags must be in the correct order. If you open element one, then element two, you must close element two before element one:

```
<el_a>    Open elements a,b, c
  <el_b>
    <el_c>
    </el_c>        Close elements c, b, a  - no error
  </el_b>
</el_a>
```

```
<el_a>          Open elements a,b, c
  <el_b>
  <el_c>
</el_a>         Close elements a,b, c - error
  </el_b>
    </el_c>
```

If an XML document adheres to these rules, it is said to be *well-formed*. A document with errors is not well-formed and the computer will refuse to show it – in marked contract to HTML, which allows programmers to make numerous errors. XML is very strict and overall this encourages a better more disciplined coding style.

Data inside a Character Data block is ignored by the XML parser. Use CDATA to include code in another language or plain text that does not need parsing.

```
<![CDATA[            Note the two square brackets.
  <html>             Include some HTML code.
  <body>
    <p>Character data</p>
  </body>
  </html>
]]>                  Close both brackets.
```

Some characters are forbidden inside XML elements because they would confuse the computer, e.g. the open and close brackets used around tags. To get around this XML has built in *entities* – codes that will print the forbidden characters.

An entity consists of an ampersand, the name and a semi-colon. These are built-in:

```
&amp;        &  Ampersand
&lt;         <  Less than symbol or open bracket
&gt;         >  Greater than symbol or close bracket
&apos;       '  Apostrophe
&quot;       "  Quotation mark
```

You can display any character using a numeric entity representing the Unicode value of the character, either in decimal or hexadecimal:

```
&#42;        Base 10
&#x02F;      Precede value with an x to tell computer is base 16
```

Programmers may define their own entities in a DTD. A user-defined entity is called in the following way:

```
&entityname;
```

DTDs

For an XML document to be valid, it has to comply with rules laid down in a document type definition (DTD). In the DTD we define element names, attribute information and entities. A DTD can either be held inside a document or in an external file, and is called with a line known as the document type declaration.

The document type declaration contains the name of the DTD and its location. All external DTD filenames have the .dtd suffix. The **SYSTEM** keyword is used for DTDs that are in use on the current system, one can also use **PUBLIC** to specify a DTD anybody can refer to (i.e. the WML or XHTML DTDs). PUBLIC DTDs use a FPI (Formal Public Identifier) to describe where they reside on the Internet.

The following calls a local DTD:

```
<!DOCTYPE doc SYSTEM "doc.dtd">
```

This refers to the XHTML DTD with FPI and direct URL link:

```
<!DOCTYPE html PUBLIC "-//W3C//DTD XHTML 1.0 Transitional//EN"
"http://www.w3.org/TR/xhtml1/DTD/xhtml1-transitional.dtd">
```

An internal DTD is placed inside the XML prologue:

```
<?xml version="1.0" standalone="yes" ?>
<!DOCTYPE doc [
  <!— place element and attribute rules here —>
]>
<doccode>
<!—XML code —>
</doccode>
```

An external DTD is a collection of rules on their own without an XML prologue or DOCTYPE call.

Elements

Elements are defined by the ELEMENT keyword and a series of values, in the form:

```
<!ELEMENT nameofelement (contents)>
```

The contents may refer to the current element or child elements specified later. Content types may be set to PCDATA (i.e. text), ANY (anything) or EMPTY.

```
<!ELEMENT person (arms, legs, clothes)>     Parent and child elements
<!ELEMENT arms (#PCDATA)>                    Arms contains normal data
<!ELEMENT legs  EMPTY>                            <legs/>
```

143

```
<!ELEMENT clothes ANY>                    Can contain anything
```

Element content can be mixed. For instance you can include an element which may have either character data as a value or refer to another element:

```
<!ELEMENT name (#PCDATA | person)>Place the PCDATA part first
```

The bar is an occurrence indicator that tells the parser how elements should be used. In mixed content we only use two (| and *). You can use the following symbols when specifying element definitions:

,	All elements included in order (element1,element2, element3)
|	Use one or the other (element1|element2)
+	Use once or many times
*	Element optional or can be used as many times as user wants
?	Optional or use once only

An occurrence indicator may apply to a single element or several if placed outside the brackets:

```
<!ELEMENT city (name+, brief+, (fun| places| comments|image)*)>
```

Attributes

Attributes are specified with the ATTLIST command:

```
<!ATTLIST tagname  attributename (type) value >
```

A single element can contain any number of attributes, with one ATTLIST for each.

The attribute has to have a specific type that describes the data it holds. This can be set to any of the following possibilities:

CDATA   Character data that obeys XML rules (use entities for forbidden characters)

Enumerated Attribute has a choice of values (val1 |val2)

ID   Identity code for attribute

IDREF/S   Attribute set to value of one or more elements

NMTOKEN/S   Value must be valid XML name (no spaces or forbidden characters)

ENTITY   Call external data

NOTATION   Unparsed data (i.e. multimedia files)

The value can be a default string, or one of the following options:

#REQUIRED   Attribute must always be used with element

#IMPLIED   Attribute optional

#FIXED "value"   Attribute must have fixed value if used

Hence a *café* element might have attributes similar to those below. The *location* attribute must always feature; if *sells* is used it has to have one of three values (enumerated) and finally *vat* will be the same all the time (17.5%):

```
<!ATTLIST cafe location CDATA #REQUIRED >
<!ATTLIST cafe sells  (alcohol | coffee |food)>
<!ATTLIST cafe vat CDATA #FIXED "17.5" >
```

Entities

To define an entity in your DTD, use the ENTITY keyword together with an entity name and the value in a string. An internal entity covers text strings (for example often used names and titles) whereas external entities reference information held outside the document:

```
<!ENTITY dtdnam "Document Type Defintion">   Use &dtdnam; to show text
```

Calling an external unparsed entity involves using the **NOTATION** call to set the type of file used:

```
<!ENTITY file SYSTEM "media.wav" NDATA wav>
<!NOTATION wav SYSTEM "audio/x-wav">
```

Take note

This summary is not intended to be a comprehensive reference. If you want to know the full scope of each XML technology, the best place to go is the World Wide Web Consortium's site at http://www.w3.org/ where complete references are available.

CSS overview

Cascading Style Sheets are stored in a text file with the extension *.CSS*. To call a stylesheet from an XML document, include a line like this in the prologue:

```
<?xml-stylesheet  href="stylesheetname.css" type="text/css" ?>
```

A stylesheet consists of a series of rules comprising a *selector* (the element having style applied to it) and the *declaration* (properties to be altered and their values):

```
Selector {property: value}
```

Rules have a chain of inheritance where a child element inherits the value of the parent element surrounding it unless the stylesheet states otherwise.

The following rule will place a border around data from the element called *para*. The example underneath it will display title text in the Arial font:

```
/* Comment lines written in this format */
para {border: 1px solid black}
title {font-family: Arial}
```

Selectors can be grouped, applying the same rule to several elements. A selector can contain one or many *property:value* pairs, so long as each one is separated by a semi-colon. You can format the rules all together or have one per line:

```
/* Apply rules to title, body and para elements. */
title,body,para {  font-family: Arial }
/* property definitions can be written in a continuous line like this */
bigpara {font-family: Arial; font-size: 20px; display:block; border: 2px solid
black}
/* or spaced out for easier reading */
bigpara {
font-family: Arial;
font-size: 20px;
display:block;
border: 2px solid black
}
```

Values

Values in a stylesheet have a number of possible unit types:

px	pixels	**in**	inches
mm	millimetres	**cm**	centimetres
pt	points (72 to an inch)	**pc**	pica (1 pica = 12 points)
em	relative to font size (see below)		

One **em** is equivalent to the present font size. Therefore if a font is 40 pixels high and the next selector has a value of 2 em, those letters will be 80 pixels high.

You can also give relative sizes using percentage values.

```
title { font-size: 20pt}
bigtitle {font-size: 200%}
```

Text size can be set with a keyword, e.g. *small*, *medium*, *large*, *smaller* and *larger*.

```
bodytext {font-size: medium}
```

Colour values are given either using a hexadecimal number with a RGB scale or a standard name such as red, blue, brown, etc.):

```
background-color: red;
color #FF0000;
```

Useful properties

We can think of the element data as text placed in a box. This box can have a border around it, the colours changed, or its position altered on the screen.

In our examples we use the value *block*. This makes the text appear in a box with line breaks at the beginning and end. We can also set display to *inline* (no line feeds), *table* (shown in a table), *list-item* and *none* (element is not shown).

These are the main properties for manipulating fonts:

font-family: general font name (serif, monospace, etc.) or family name (Verdana,Arial)

font-style: values *italic* or *normal*

font-size: size (16px, 72 pt)

font-weight: *normal*, *bold* or a value from 1-900

text-decoration: *underline*, *overline*, *line-through* or *none*

text-transform: *uppercase*, *lowercase* or *capitalise* text

Altering the spacing of text inside the element box is done with the following:

letter-spacing: value for spacing between individual letters

word-spacing: value for spacing between words

white-space: *normal*, *nowrap* (no word wrap), *pre* (preserves space)

line-height: vertical spacing value

text-indent: indent value for blocks of text

text-align: either left, right, center or justify

margin-top, **margin-bottom**, **margin-left**, **margin-right:** values for margin surrounding text box

padding-top, **padding-bottom**, **padding-left**, **padding-right:** space between element text and border

border-width: the border around the text box

border-style: solid, double, dotted, dash, groove, inset, outset

General colour properties:

color: element colour

background-color: colour of text box

border-color: can place border width, style and color in one rule

Text is positioned on screen using these properties. Programmers should be very careful when using direct positioning as results can differ between browser applications:

position: absolute or relative

left: horizontal distance value

top: vertical distance value

The following general tags affect how your elements look on screen and whether you have a background picture or not:

visibility: if set to visible element is shown, set to hidden and the element vanishes

z-index: order of overlap (similar to SMIL).

background-image: url of picture (JPEG or GIF)

background-repeat: repeat, repeat-x,repeat-y, no-repeat

background-attachment: image can either be fixed or scroll

height: element height

width: element width

SMIL overview

If you have RealPlayer and a relatively fast Internet connection you can see an excellent example of SMIL in action on the W3C page '*Finding your way at W3C*' (http://www.w3.org/2002/03/new-to-w3c). Click on the picture of Tim Berners Lee (the originator of the Web). You will see a short monologue of the man himself speaking, while subtitles in three different languages appear underneath the video.

Structure

A SMIL file is structured as follows:

```
<smil>
  <head>
    Place identifying information here and layout details...
  </head>
  <body>
    Place audio/video data here...
  </body>
</smil>
```

The header contains information about the presentation, and possible details of screen layout (if the browser window is split into sections). Actual multimedia content is placed between the body tags.

Header

In a SMIL header we can store meta information about the presentation. The format is very similar to HTML (**<meta name="nameofdata" content="sometext" />**). Examples include the name of the presentation's author, the title and keywords:

```
<meta name="title" content="A fun presentation" />
<meta name="author" content="Wilbur and Tammy" />
<meta name="keywords" content="SMIL, video, audio" />
```

The header is the place to define your layout. This consists of a series of regions, each identified with a name using the **id** attribute. Setting up regions is done in the following way:

```
<layout>
<root-layout background-color="black" width="700" height="280"/>
<region  id="back" top="0" left="0" width="380" height="280" fit="fill" z-index="0"/>
<region  id="video" top="60" left="390" width="300" height="220" z-index="1"/>
</layout>
```

The **layout** element contains an initial **root-layout** element, which specifies the boundaries of the browser window. In the example the window is 700 pixels across by 280 high, with a black background.

Next, two regions are defined in the **region** elements. Each region must have an **id**, and coordinates describing its position within the window. The **back** region begins at the origin (0,0 – top left corner), and is 380 pixels across by 280 high. The **video** region begins 60 pixels from the top of the window and 390 pixels across, and is 300 × 220 pixels. Hence the back region covers the first half of the browser, there is a 10 pixel gap, then the video window follows, which is offset 60 pixels down from the top. If regions are placed over each other, we set the **z-index** attribute. A region with a high z-index takes priority over a lower index. So if two regions are in the same place, the higher indexed region will be the only one the user can see.

The **fit** attribute can have several values. If set to *fill*, whatever is placed inside the area is scaled to fill the whole region, even if it is distorted in the process. If fit has the value *meet*, media are scaled to fit as much of the region as possible, but their aspect ratio is preserved. If the value *hidden* is used (default) the clip is shown without any alterations, starting at the top of the current region.

Body and content

Content is described by using the source tag with file type and duration attributes. The main media file types are **img** (image), **video**, **audio**, **text**, **textstream** and **animation**. You can specify the time the media is shown for (the **dur** attribute), and a delay before playback or display starts (using **begin**). The source specifies the location of the file and can either be a URL or file link if the SMIL code and media are held on the same computer:

```
<img src="image1.jpg" dur="10s"/>        Show picture for 10 seconds
<video src="demo.mpg" dur="40s"/>        Play video for 40 seconds
<audio src="fx.wav" begin="10s" dur="5s"/>   Wait 10 seconds then play
```

Note that media elements should always be closed with the / symbol, to make them compliant with XML rules. To display content within a region, you must add the region attribute with an appropriate name.

```
<video src="vidtest.rm" region="video" />    Display in video region
<img src="edin.jpg" region="back" />         Display in back region
```

You can do basic hyperlinks by using the **<a href>** element. In this example, when the user clicks on the video window, the link starts up a second video. If using an Internet address rather than a file link, you must specify the full address, including the protocol (usually **http://**, but in the case of streaming video also **rtsp://**).

```
<a href="vidtest2.rm" region="backregion">        Link to video two
<video src="vidtest.rm" region="backregion"/>      Video currently playing
</a>
```

Time

Time information is represented in two ways. Multimedia data can be shown in a sequence (**<seq></seq>**) or execute in parallel with other content (**<par></par>**). The **repeat** attribute tells the computer how many times a particular media element should be shown, and can either be a numerical value or set to *indefinite*, which makes the sequence loop until forced to end.

```
<seq repeat="5">
<img src="pica.gif" dur="10s"/>      Displays pictures one after the other
<img src="picb.gif" dur="10s"/>      and repeat sequence five times.
<img src="picc.gif" dur="10s"/>
</seq>
<par repeat="indefinite">
<video src="movie.mpg">              Plays music and video at the same time
<audio src="soundtrack.mp3">         and loop the sequence indefinitely.
</par>
```

In the above examples, units of time are represented in the: Time=**"x seconds"** format. SMIL also allows time to be represented either by unit, or in a digital clock format (HH:MM:SS). The following are all valid time values.

```
<img src="picture.jpg" dur="00:10:00" />      Show for 10 minutes.
<img src="picture.jpg" dur="01:00:00" />      Show for one hour.
<img src="picture.jpg" dur="00:00:20" />      Show for 20 seconds.
<img src="picture.jpg" dur="03:00" />         Show for three minutes.
<img src="picture.jpg" dur="1min" />          Show for one minute.
<img src="picture.jpg" dur="5s" />            Show for five seconds.
<img src="picture.jpg" dur="2h" />            Show for two hours.
```

WML overview

Full documentation on WML is available from the WAP Forum site (now renamed the Open Mobile Alliance). For example, you can download the entire specifications for WAP 1.2 at http://www.wapforum.org/what/technical_1_2.htm.

A WML *deck* consists of a set of *cards*. Decks typically follow the XML format:

```
<?xml version="1.0"?>
<!DOCTYPE wml PUBLIC "-//WAPFORUM//DTD WML 1.2//EN"
"http://www.wapforum.org/DTD/wml_1.2.xml">
<wml>
<card>
<!—include content here—>
</card>
<card>
<!—more content—>
</card>
</wml>
```

A WML file begins with an XML prologue describing the XML version (at present 1.0) and a link to the WML document type definition (version 1.2 here, but 2.0 will be the norm in future). Inside the root element **<wml>** are the card definitions.

Cards and text

A card tag contains several attributes. The ID attribute is used for linking, when we need to identify each card. Each card can have a title, shown at the top of the display:

```
<card id="cardone" title="Test">
<p> Hello! </p>
<p> Text on  <br/> two lines. <p>
</card>
```

Generally text is displayed using the **<p>** (paragraph) tag. You may set the **align** attribute for left, right or centre aligned text. The **mode** attribute is either *wrap* (word wrap to next line) or *nowrap* (continue text off screen). You can force text onto a new line by using the line break **
** tag.

`<p align="center" mode="wrap"> Some text</p>`	Centre text with wrap
`<p align="left" mode="wrap"> Some text</p>`	Default text mode
`<p align="right" mode="nowrap"> Some text</p>`	Right align with no wrap

Other modes of display for text are **<b>**, **<i>**,**<u>**, **<big>**, **<small>**, **<em>** (emphasized) and **<strong>**:

```
<b> Bold Text </b>
<i> Italics </i>
<u> Underlined </u>
<big> Big text </big>
```

WML includes facilities for character entities similar to XML (and includes the non-breaking space entity used for added extra space between text), for example:

```
&amp;      Show ampersand
      Insert space
&quot;     Insert quotation mark
```

You can create a table in WML for holding information in a strictly formatted way. The table element can have an optional title but must specify the number of columns, each defined with the <td> element. Individual columns are held inside row tags. The following example creates a table of two columns and two rows.

```
<table columns="2" title="Demo Table">
  <tr>
    <td> Cell 1 </td>
    <td> Cell 2 </td>
  </tr>
  <tr>
    <td> Cell 3 </td>
    <td> Cell 4 </td>
  </tr>
</table>
```

To insert a picture, use the **<img src>** element. Presently the most supported format with WAP is the monochrome WBMP format, although newer phones can display colour pictures in PNG (Portable Network Graphic), GIF (Graphics Interchange Format) and JPEG (Joint Photographic Experts Group). The **alt** attribute specifies alternative text if the user-agent cannot load the image.

```
<img src="logo.wbmp" alt="Logo picture" />
```

You can specify the size of the image in pixels, with the **width** and **height** attributes. This is used if you want precise control over how your screen should look, but can also be utilised in animation effects (i.e. by changing the attributes and showing the same picture on different cards using a timer, thus making it alter in size from frame to frame). Browser support is somewhat sketchy, so remember to test any effects before you let people connect to your pages.

```
<img src="logo.wbmp" width="140" height="60" />
```

Hyperlinks are available through the **\<a href>** element. You may link to another page or site by specifying the full URL, or you can link to another card in your deck by prefixing the card ID name with a hash symbol as shown below:

```
<a  href="http://www.google.com">Search</a>      Link to external site
<a href="#two">Next card </a>                     Link to card with ID "two"
<a href="mysitewap.wml">WAP Site</a>             Link to new deck locally
```

Events

WML is event-driven, i.e. the browser performs actions when something happens such as a key is pressed, or a timer elapses. When an event occurs the user-agent performs a *task*, called by a command such as **\<go>** (initiate page navigation) or **\<do>** (call a general event). A typical element that calls a task is **\<anchor>**. Instead of using **\<a>** (which is a subset of anchor), using **\<anchor>** allows the programmer to specify a task if a link is clicked on:

```
<anchor>
Click Here
<go href="#card" />      Jump to a card when clicked on.
</anchor>
<anchor>
Go back
<prev/>                  Go back to previous page when clicked on.
</anchor>
```

The **\<do>** element has several possible values (events can be used as either full elements or as attributes of another element). It can be used to go back a page (*prev*), display a help page (*help*), acknowledge an operation (*accept*), request optional information (*options*) and reset a card (*reset*). Typically these events are mapped to one of the option buttons on a WAP phone. We specify the values in the type attribute, along with a label:

```
<do type="accept" label="Okay">    When button pressed
<go href="check.wml" />            jump to check.wml.
</do>
<do type="prev" label="Go Back">   Go back a page.
<prev/>
</do>
```

The **\<prev>** element may also contain element data, such as variable settings, hence does not need to be empty all the time.

Some events are called from within the card element using the event name as an attribute. These are **onenterforward** (when you navigate to a card), **onenterbackward** (coming to a card via a prev operation). Events may also be called using the **onevent** element with **type** attribute. In the examples below the user-agent redirects to the URL as soon as the page is loaded. The second example redirects to another card when somebody goes back to the page. This might be used to stop a user revisiting a page they only need to see once (i.e. a title screen):

```
<card id="two" onenterforward="http://www.google.com">
<card id="one" onenterbackward="#page">
```

We can use **onevent** within the card to do a similar redirect:

```
<onevent type="onenterforward">
<go href="http://www.google.com" />
</onevent>
```

Pieces of event code can be repeated in every card on a deck by use of the **<template>** element. If you place your template code at the beginning of a WML file, just after the **<wml>** tag it is available to all cards:

```
<wml>
<template>
<do type="prev" label="Back">        Previous Option on all cards.
<prev/>
</do>
</template>
<card>
Code here
</card>
</wml>
```

Timed events in WML are built using a **timer** element and the **ontimer** event. You set ontimer to go to a specific link when the timer hits zero, then place a line in the code listing a value to count down from (in tenths of a second).

```
<card id="one" ontimer="#two">        Jump to card two
<timer value="20"/>                   after two seconds.
<p>card one</p>
</card>
<card id="two">
<p> card two </p>
</card>
```

Variables and input

Variable values can either come from user inputs or be set directly with **setvar**. This element has two attributes, variable **name** and **value** and must be placed inside a task call such as **<do>** or **<anchor>** otherwise an error results:

```
<do type="prev">
<prev>
<setvar name="greet" value="HELLO!" /> String with value "HELLO"
</prev>
</do>
```

You can also surround the variable setting with the **<refresh>** element if you wish to update the page (i.e. so a new value will be shown).

Variable contents are displayed by placing the name within brackets and prefixing it with a dollar sign:

```
<p> $(value) </p>
```

The user has several means of inputting some data:

Input a string called *name*; the value is a default shown in the text box:

```
<input name="name" value="Steph"/>
```

Input a password (shown in asterisks):

```
<input name="pass" type="password"/>
```

Input some data in a 10 character long textbox with a maximum string size of 10 characters:

```
<input name="num"  size="10" maxlength="10"/>
```

A list of selections can be used instead:

```
<select name="choose">          Creates a variable called 'choose'.
<option value="UK">UK</option>   With the selection result as
<option value="US">USA</option>  its value.
</select>
```

The names of the user inputs are treated like normal variables. The **onpick** event is useful for causing the browser to do something when the user makes a selection, in this case jumping to a page depending on the country chosen:

```
<select name="choose">
<option value="UK" onpick="#UK">UK</option>
<option value="US" onpick="#US">USA</option>
</select>
```

Answers to exercises

Chapter 1

1   We know the message consists of two words as there is a character 32 (space) in the middle. We also know upper case letters in ASCII begin with A at 65, B at 66 and so on. Therefore the message is:

    SIMPLE XML

2   An XML document is extensible in the sense that you define your own tags, as long as you tell the computer what each tag means in a document type definition, then you can have as many as you want.

3   XML defines the meaning of data, HTML describes how a document should be viewed, but does not say anything about the meaning of the information contained in the document. On its own an XML document does not do much, so other mechanisms have to be utilised to create formatted output.

4   You may not want people to be able to read your electronic documents. If your old system stored data in a proprietary format a casual observer glancing at a file may not be able to make much sense of it. Information can be gleaned from XML even if you know almost nothing about computers. For information on databases (i.e. medical or financial information) special care must be taken to make sure only the right people see the files. Some form of encryption will be needed to make sure the data is unreadable while it travels from computer to computer.

Chapter 2

1   A well-formed document complies with the syntactical rules of XML. Elements should be nested correctly (<el> <two>data </two> </el>, <u>not</u> <el><two>data </el></two>), all elements must have opening and closing tags (or combine both into a single close tag), a root element exists and should contain all the other elements and so on. A well-formed document can be used on its own without the need for a Document Type Definition. If a well-formed XML document uses a DTD and is consistent with the structure laid down in the DTD, it is said to be valid.

2   You will get a parsing error as the ampersand is a restricted character. To get the code to work, you need to use the entity *amp* instead:

    <greeting> To Jimmy & Suzie </greeting>

3   This code fragment has quite a few errors:

```
<?xml version="1.0"? encoding="UTF">
<code>
<title><bold> My Programming Page </title></bold>
<lang favourite="list>
<prog> C & C++ </prog>
<prog> PERL   </prog>
<prog> Java <prog/>
</lang>
<code>
<xml>
```

In first line, question mark should be at end and encoding should read "UTF-8"

The tags **<title>** and **<bold>** are not nested correctly.

Lang favourite attribute needs a final quote mark around the word "list".

An ampersand is used. This should be replaced with the correct entity (&).

In Java line, **<prog/>** should be **</prog>**

The root element **<code>** should be closed at the end **</code>**.

The **<xml>** tag at the end is incorrect. You do not have to close an XML document with an **<xml>** tag. The tag is actually in error because it is not even closed.

Chapter 3

1   The DTD fragment below has an incorrect round bracket in the first line (it should be square). The element *planet* contains the parameter CDATA, which should be PCDATA. The element *star* is contradictory; if it is an empty element, why would it include extra data? Either PCDATA or EMPTY must be removed.

```
<!DOCTYPE space (
<!ELEMENT space (star*,planet+, satellite*)>
<!ELEMENT star  (#PCDATA) EMPTY>
<!ELEMENT planet (#CDATA)>
<!ELEMENT satellite (#PCDATA)>
]>
```

2   The element shown in the question is not the correct one, which shows *visualbasic* as element data, when it really should be an attribute. If we look at the DTD line:

```
<!ATTLIST program visualbasic (ver4| ver5 | ver6) #REQUIRED >
```

We can see the *visualbasic* attribute requires a version parameter. Hence a correct XML element call would be:

```
<program visualbasic="ver4"> You have VB 4 </program>
```

3   The element is empty, so should consist of a single tag that closes itself: **<brain/>**

Chapter 4

1   Either the elements referred to by the errant lines will not appear with the correct formatting, or the entire stylesheet will be ignored by the browser.

2   First, the background URL will link to the picture, but we also have to tell the browser whether the picture is on its own, or if it tiles across the screen. If the **background-repeat** property is set to *no*, the picture will appear only once. We then have to enter the size of the picture. Finally, we can produce a collage effect by placing images at different positions. This example is very simple – the XML tags tell the browser to show an image, and the stylesheet (*style.xml*) displays them:

xml file:

```
<?xml version="1.0"?>
<?xml-stylesheet  href="style.css" type="text/css" ?>
<collage>
<pic/>
<pic2/>
<pic3/>
</collage>
```

style.xml

```
pic {background-image: url("london.jpg"); background-repeat:no-repeat;
    height:280px; width:380px; }
pic2 {background-image: url("liverpool.jpg"); position:absolute; left:300px;
top:40px; background-repeat:no-repeat; height:300px; width:400px; }
pic3 {background-image: url("cardiff.jpg"); position:absolute; left:200px;
top:240px; background-repeat:no-repeat; height:320px; width:360px; }
```

You could add as many pictures as you want, or place coloured text on screen as well. The versatility of CSS allows you numerous choices.

3   Once again, it is entirely up to you how you set out your pages. The example below aims for simple coloured text with a picture at the bottom of the screen. For your answer you may have used indented, rather than aligned text, or played around with

background images. Note that as the picture name is embedded inside the stylesheet, you would need to have different elements for different pictures. This kind of shortcoming is the sort of thing XSL is good for.

guide.xml

```
<?xml version="1.0"?>
<!DOCTYPE city SYSTEM "city.dtd">
<?xml-stylesheet  href="guide.css" type="text/css" ?>
<city>
<general> &title; </general>
<name location="London"> London </name>
<brief>London is the capital city of the UK</brief>
<fun>Visit Madame Tussauds</fun>
<fun>Visit the science museum</fun>
<places>Buckingham Palace</places>
<places>The Houses of Parliament</places>
<comments>One of the world's top cities.</comments>
<image/>
</city>
```

guide.css

```
general {color:blue; text-align:center; display:block; }
name {color:red; font-family:Arial; font-size:40px; text-align:center;
display:block; }
brief {color:black; font-family:Arial; font-size:18px; text-align:center;
display:block; }
fun {color:black; font-family:Arial; font-size:16px; text-align:center;
display:block; }
places {color: gray; font-family:Arial; font-size:12px; text-align:center;
display:block; }
comments {color: black; font-family:Arial; font-size:10px; text-align:center;
display:block; }
image { background-image: url("London.jpg"); display:block; background-
repeat:no-repeat; height:300px; width:420px;  }
```

Chapter 5

1   The document refers to some kind of company or university department devoted to computer security. The **<title>** element is used both for the title of people (Miss Smith, Professor Challenger), and the title of computer science papers. We would therefore use separate namespaces for the two elements, as the code below shows.

```
<?xml version="1.0"?>
<compsec xmlns: nm="www.theuniversitysite/compsec/people"
xmlns: pr="www.theuniversitysite/compsec/papers">
<people>
<nm:title>Doctor</title>
<nm:title>Professor</title>
<nm:title>Mr</title>
<nm:title>Miss</title>
</people>
<papers>
<pr:title>New security vulnerabilities</title>
<pr:title>Stopping Computer Worms</title>
<pr:title>Denial of Service prevention</title>
<pr:title>Quantum Cryptography</title>
</papers>
</compsec>
```

2   The schema language has more features than the traditional DTD and is becoming
     the standard for describing XML documents in many areas. Furthermore a DTD
     tends to stick to a very simple data-type (CDATA), but schemas support more
     advanced typing. XML is increasingly being used for exchanging information
     between databases and files, so having fine control over the kinds of data allowed
     in documents is essential.

3   The following schema includes all the elements and tags used in the city guide pages:

```
<?xml version="1.0" encoding="UTF-8"?>
<xs:schema xmlns:xs="http://www.w3.org/2001/XMLSchema"
elementFormDefault="qualified">
<xs:element name="brief" type="xs:string"/>
<xs:element name="city">
<xs:complexType>
<xs:sequence>
<xs:element ref="general"/>
<xs:element ref="name" maxOccurs="unbounded"/>
<xs:element ref="brief" maxOccurs="unbounded"/>
<xs:choice minOccurs="0" maxOccurs="unbounded">
<xs:element ref="fun"/>
<xs:element ref="places"/>
<xs:element ref="comments"/>
<xs:element ref="image"/>
</xs:choice>
```

```
</xs:sequence>
</xs:complexType>
</xs:element>
<xs:element name="comments" type="xs:string"/>
<xs:element name="fun" type="xs:string"/>
<xs:element name="general" type="xs:string"/>
<xs:element name="image" type="xs:string"/>
<xs:element name="name">
<xs:complexType>
<xs:simpleContent>
<xs:extension base="xs:string">
<xs:attribute name="population" type="xs:string" default="unknown"/>
<xs:attribute name="location" type="xs:string" use="required"/>
<xs:attribute name="rating" type="xs:string" default="outoften"/>
</xs:extension>
</xs:simpleContent>
</xs:complexType>
</xs:element>
<xs:element name="places" type="xs:string"/>
</xs:schema>
```

Chapter 6

1 Cascading Style Sheets are about adding presentation information to a document. XSLT can convert entire documents from one format to another. With CSS the XML document stays as an XML document, and the browser adds in the formatting data based on the CSS properties.

If XSLT is used, the document is transformed from the XML source into a result document in another format. Hence an XML document on the server may end up as a WML document on your mobile phone, or a XHTML document on your PDA. XSLT can also manipulate document elements (i.e. sorting them, removing elements) in a much more comprehensive way than CSS.

2 If we transform documents on the server users will receive the plain processed data, and do not need a powerful browser to see it. For example Internet Explorer has an inbuilt parser that can handle XML conversions, but a WAP user-agent has to be fitted into a tiny memory footprint so would not be able to run something the size of XSLT. We can for that reason also create several versions of our data each in a different web language; perhaps even have customised versions for individual browsers. The web server can read what type of browser the client is using and redirect them to the correct pages. A possible disadvantage of this would be that the server would need extra processing capacity to do all the XML transformations, however the amount needed on average sites would be negligible.

3   We have opted here for a simple colourful display, not dissimilar to the results of the CSS exercise. We start with the headings displayed in large letters. Following on we have placed the repeated elements inside a table. The top of the table contains the **\<fun\>** entries, followed by a ruled line, and then the **\<places\>** information. The table border is set to zero so the visitor merely sees formatted text. Finally, if the image attribute contains a filename, that is turned into a **\<img src\>** HTML tag and the relevant picture loaded:

Xml page:

```
<?xml version="1.0"?>
<!DOCTYPE city SYSTEM "city.dtd">
<?xml-stylesheet type="text/xsl" href="output.xsl"?>
<city>
<general> &title; </general>
<name location="London"> London </name>
<brief>London is the capital city of the UK</brief>
<fun>Visit Madame Tussauds</fun>
<fun>Visit the science museum</fun>
<places>Buckingham Palace</places>
<places>The Houses of Parliament</places>
<comments>One of the world's top cities.</comments>
<image>stpauls.jpg</image>
</city>
```

output.xsl file

```
<?xml version="1.0" encoding="utf-8"?>
<xsl:stylesheet version="2.0" xmlns:xsl="http://www.w3.org/1999/XSL/Transform">
<xsl:template match="/">
<html>
<head> XSL Demo </head>
<body>
<center>
<p><font size="+2" face="Arial, Helvetica, sans-serif">
<xsl:value-of select="city/general"/> </font></p>
<p><font size="+4" color="red" face="Arial, Helvetica, sans-serif">
<xsl:value-of select="city/name"/> </font></p>
<p><font size="+3" color="blue" face="Arial, Helvetica, sans-serif">
```

```
<xsl:value-of select="city/brief"/> </font> </p>
<table width="400" border="0">
<tr><td align="center"><u>Fun things To Do In Town</u> </td></tr>
<xsl:for-each select="city/fun">
<tr> <td align="center"><font size="+3">
<xsl:value-of select="." /> </font></td>
</tr>
</xsl:for-each>
<tr><td><hr/></td></tr>
<tr><td align="center"><u>Places</u> </td></tr>
<xsl:for-each select="city/places">
<tr> <td align="center"><font size="+3">
<xsl:value-of select="." /> </font></td>
</tr>
</xsl:for-each>
</table>
<br/>
<p><font size="+3" color="blue" face="Arial, Helvetica, sans-serif">
<xsl:value-of select="city/comments"/> </font> </p>
<hr/>
<img>
  <xsl:attribute name="src">
  <xsl:value-of select="city/image" />
  </xsl:attribute>
  <xsl:attribute name="alt">
  Picture of city
  </xsl:attribute>
</img>
<hr/>
</center>
</body>
</html>
</xsl:template>
</xsl:stylesheet>
```

Chapter 7

1   Code akin to the following adds an XLink inside the links element. Note that when
     you enter the xref web address, make sure you place the full address (including the
     http://www) or else the browser will assume it is a link to a local file.

```
<?xml version="1.0"?>
<!DOCTYPE city SYSTEM "city.dtd">
```

```
<!— Make sure DTD is in same folder as file —>
<city>
<name location="London"> London </name>
<comments> Stick information here </comments>
<links xmlns:xlink="http://www.w3.org/1999/xlink" >
<xlink:hyperlink xlink:type="simple"
xlink:href="http://www.nhm.ac.uk/"
xlink:title="Natural History Museum"
xlink:role="Museum"
xlink:show="replace"
xlink:actuate="onClick">National History Museum</xlink:hyperlink>
</links>
</city>
```

2   An obvious problem is that the actuate attribute makes it very easy to add pop-up ads to web pages. By setting actuate="onload" and show="new", a new window would pop up every time you went to the site. This is quite useful if used in moderation, but is bound to be abused by advertisement-obsessed web designers.

A further problem is the XLink specification itself seems to allow self-referential links. As it stands there is nothing to stop you from making a page link to itself. If you set the page to open another one with the same hyperlink when the initial page is visited, the computer may well keep opening new windows until it crashes!

Say the code below can be found at the hypothetical site: **www.address-of-this-page.co.uk**. When anyone with an XLink-compatible browser visits the page, it will open a new browser window at the same page, which will open another one, and so on until the program is halted. This could be very annoying and may not be stopped by anti-pop-up programs that look for embedded JavaScript, not an XLink.

```
<?xml version="1.0"?>
<media xmlns:xlink="http://www.w3.org/1999/xlink" >
<xlink:hyperlink xlink:type="simple"
xlink:href="www.address-of-this-page.co.uk"
xlink:title="Ad infinitum test"
xlink:role="Test only"
xlink:show="new"
xlink:actuate="onLoad">Beware!!</xlink:hyperlink>
</media>
```

XLink is not yet supported by most browsers and shortcomings of this sort should be amended by the time popular web sites start using the XML linking language.

3 The XHTML code contains mistakes similar to those in the Chapter 2 exercise. It is composed of a table with cells holding the names of books and their authors. Lines such as the following exist throughout:

`<td><font color="#003366>Idoru</font></td>`

All attributes must be surrounded by quotes, so this font colour is in error. The word *colour* is use as an attribute in two lines. The US spelling (color) should be used.

This line has incorrect nesting of tags: **<td>Title</td></td>**

XHTML pages should end with **</html>**, not **</xml>**.

Chapter 8

1 In the following example, we have two regions visible. The background image is displayed in *back*, and the video in the *video* region. We set video's z-index higher so it appears over the picture, and as the video window is smaller, it is offset slightly so it appears in the center of the image. For the test we use a RM movie, which is the RealNetworks video streaming file format.

```
<smil>
<head>
<layout>
<root-layout background-color="black" width="400" height="300"/>
<region id="back" top="0" left="0" width="400" height="300" z-index="0"/>
<region id="video" top="30" left="40" width="300" height="220" z-index="1"/>
</layout>
</head>
<body>
<seq>
<par>
<img src="picture.jpg" region="back" fill="freeze" />
<video src="vidtest.rm" region="video" />
</par>
</seq>
</body>
</smil>
```

2 We set up two regions again, as with question 1. The difference is that this time both regions are separate. The video stream is sent to one, and a sequence of pictures sent to the other. Images alternate on a 10 second timer while the video runs in parallel.

```
<smil>
<head>
<layout>
<root-layout background-color="black" width="700" height="280"/>
<region id="back" top="0" left="0" width="380" height="280" />
<region id="video" top="30" left="390" width="300" height="220" />
</layout>
</head>
<body>
<seq>
<par>
<video src="vidtest.rm" region="video" />
<seq repeat="indefinite">
<img src="edin.jpg" region="back" fill="freeze" dur="10s" />
<img src="londoneye.jpg" region="back" fill="freeze" dur="10s"/>
<img src="liverpool.jpg" region="back" fill="freeze" dur="10s" />
</seq>
</par>
</seq>
</body>
</smil>
```

3   This feed is the kind of thing we might use:

```
<?xml version="1.0"?>
<rss version="2.0">
<channel>
<title> Travel News </title>
<link> http://www.city-test-site.com </link>
<description> XML Made Simple City Guide </description>
<language>en-gb</language>
<item>
<title> City News </title>
<link> http://www.city-test-site.com/news  </link>
<description>Latest travel news</description>
<category>Travel</category>
</item>
<item>
<title> Weather </title>
<link> http://www.city-test-site.com/weather </link>
<description>The weather in your area.</description>
<category>Travel</category>
</item>
</channel>
</rss>
```

4. When using RSS all the visitor needs is a link to the RSS file. They do not have to give any personal information. RSS is therefore a more anonymous way of keeping people up to date about changes to your site. If the user has a RSS link in their news reader program, they can simply delete the link if they do not wish to keep receiving feeds. With an email newsletter you have to go through an unsubscribe procedure, and some personal data is held on site (name, email address, etc.)

Chapter 9

1   Initially we need to draw several frames for our animation. For the example here, we created three 100 × 100 bitmaps each of which featured the word XML in a different font size. These were later converted to WBMP format and saved as *anim1.wbmp*, *anim2.wbmp* and *anim3.wbmp*.

The code below has three cards with embedded timer events. The timer is set to count seconds down to zero. When the final timer event executes, the code jumps back to the first card and continues forever. If the user wants to exit, they must click on the *skip animation* hyperlink:

```
<?xml version="1.0"?>
<!DOCTYPE wml PUBLIC "-//WAPFORUM//DTD WML 1.2//EN"
"http://www.wapforum.org/DTD/wml_1.2.xml">
<wml>
<card id="frame1" ontimer="#frame2">
<timer value="10"/>
<img src="anim1.wbmp"/>
<br/>
<p> <a href="#skip">Skip Animation</a> </p>
</card>
<card id="frame2" ontimer="#frame3">
<timer value="10"/>
<img src="anim2.wbmp"/>
<br/>
<p> <a href="#skip">Skip Animation</a> </p>
</card>
<card id="frame3" ontimer="#frame1">
<timer value="10"/>
<img src="anim3.wbmp"/>
<br/>
<p> <a href="#skip">Skip Animation</a> </p>
```

```
</card>
<card id="skip">
<p align ="center"> Main Page </p>
</card>
</wml>
```

It should be noted that while you can have a lot of fun playing with timer effects and simple animations, results will vary between different mobile devices, and may not work at all. You should always try and test any pages you intend to deploy on as many phones as possible.

2   It is possible to reduce the space needed for text – at least in a limited sense. In the following example, two string variables are defined in the text card using **setvar** (note how it is embedded between the **<go>** tags), and the browser immediately jumps to the read card. The earlier variables are printed at several points in the text. Displaying a variable's contents (only stored once) takes up less space than repeating the same string several times and is useful if you have names or long words repeated many times on your page, particularly if space is at a premium. In fact, what we are doing here is much the same as happens with an XML entity:

```
<?xml version="1.0"?>
<!DOCTYPE wml PUBLIC "-//WAPFORUM//DTD WML 1.2//EN"
"http://www.wapforum.org/DTD/wml_1.2.xml">
<wml>
<card id="text" title="Space saving example">
<anchor>
<go href="#read">
<setvar name="var" value="Wireless Markup Language"/>
<setvar name="var2" value="Extensible Markup Language"/>
</go>
Read Text
</anchor>
</card>
<card id="read" title="$(var)">
<p> $(var) is a standard for the mobile Internet.
$(var) is an $(var2) application. </p>
</card>
</wml>
```

3   The design of the code is left entirely up to you, although as a guide, you must take into account the limitations of mobile screens. Users will not want to read pages of text so it is best to place links to the various categories of information on a main

page and allow the user to browse at the city data in bite-sized chunks. The following example code for London has links to four pages:

```
<?xml version="1.0"?>
<!DOCTYPE wml PUBLIC "-//WAPFORUM//DTD WML 1.2//EN"
"http://www.wapforum.org/DTD/wml_1.2.xml">
<wml>
<template>
<do type="options" label="Main">
<prev/>
</do>
</template>
<card id="London">
<p align="center"><big>LONDON</big></p>
<p>Select a link:</p>
<table columns="2">
<tr><td><a href="#facts">Facts</a></td>
<td><a href="#fun">Fun</a></td> </tr>
<tr><td><a href="#map">Map</a></td>
<td><a href="#pic">Images</a></td> </tr>
</table>
</card>
<card id="pic" title="St Pauls">
<img src="stpaul.wbmp" alt="St Pauls Cathedral"/>
</card>
<card id="map" title="Map of London">
<img src="map.wbmp" alt="Map image"/>
</card>
<card id="facts" title="Did you know?">
<p>London is the capital city of the United Kingdom, and many of the most
important centers of government and commerce are centered here.</p>
</card>
<card id="fun" title="Things to do">
<p>Why not visit the Millennium wheel, or pop along to Madame Tussauds?
London has hundreds of great places to eat and shop.</p>
</card>
</wml>
```

You will notice that we have used a new element **<template>** (see page 155). This is a useful memory-saving trick. Anything inside the template tags will be repeated on all pages in a deck. In our example, a Back button for each card. A template can hold event code, and is not meant for things such as stand-alone blocks of text.

Glossary

ASCII (*American Standard Code for Information Interchange*) A system which defines one byte codes for characters in European languages.

Attribute A parameter added to an element to specify extra information. For example in **<name first="Sarah" second="Jones">** *name* is the tag and *first* and *second* are attributes. Attributes are sometimes called *properties*.

CSS (*Cascading Style Sheets*) A way of adding format to a HTML or XML page using standardised commands for colours, fonts and positioning.

DOM (*Document Object Model*) Envisions an XML document as a tree structure of elements and allows programmers to access any element using a language of their choice.

DTD (*Document Type Definition*) A file that describes the element and attribute rules for an XML document. If the XML obeys the rules of the DTD it is said to be valid.

Element All the information held between a start and end tag in XML. All XML documents contain at least one element (the root) which acts as a container for the other elements.

Encryption A process by which information is encoded so that only authorised persons can decode and use it. Computers use sophisticated mathematical techniques to securely encrypt data.

Entity A shortcut code for a longer string of characters. Entities can be used to replace repeating strings with the shorter codes, thus reducing typing. A *character entity* is a code used to print a character forbidden in XML documents.

HTML (*HyperText Markup Language*) The standard language for the World Wide Web. Documents are defined as text files containing tags which describe how they should look on screen and link to each other.

HTTP (*HyperText Transfer Protocol*) The communications protocol used by the World Wide Web.

Hypertext The system of electronic links that allows a person to travel from one document to another. A hyperlink that connects to another part of the same document is called an anchor.

IP address The *Internet Protocol* address identifies computers on the network and consists of four numbers (from 0-255) separated by dots: 127.0.0.1 is a special address called *localhost* and always refers to the computer you are currently using.

MathML An XML application for producing mathematical notation in documents.

Metalanguage A language that describes another language, e.g. XML is used to describe other XML languages such as SMIL or WML. *Metadata* is data describing other data – i.e. meta tags that describe the page content in HTML.

MIME (*Multipurpose Internet Mail Extensions*) Enable web servers to handle file types other than HTML or plain text (e.g. streaming video or WML pages); also enable e-mails to include non-text data.

Namespace A system of matching elements to a DTDs. Allows elements with the same name (but defined in different DTDs) to be accessed in XML documents.

Protocol A strictly-defined specification for sending data between electronic devices. The Internet uses a variety of different protocols, the main ones being HTTP and FTP (File Transfer Protocol, used to upload files to a server).

RSS (*Rich Site Summary* and also *Really Simple Syndication*) A method of letting visitors get updated information from your web site using XML. Often used for news feeds and by weblog writers to make their content more widely available.

SAX (*Simple API for XML*) A system for manipulation of XML document elements. Works on the basis of scanning a document bit by bit rather than the DOM method of seeing the document as a whole structure.

SMIL (*Synchronized Multimedia Implementation Language*) An XML application for handling multimedia content on the Internet. As yet is it not supported widely, but is gradually gaining more acceptance by the computing community.

SOAP (*Simple Object Access Protocol*) A way for applications to communicate across a HTTP-based network using XML messages.

Streaming A way of sending audio visual information piece by piece in a data stream rather than downloaded in its entirety. Popular formats include RealAudio/ Video and Windows Media streaming.

SVG (*Scalable Vector Graphics*) an XML system for producing 2D drawings in Web pages.

Tree A common data structure which consists of a root element with further elements (called nodes) branching off it.

Unicode A system where two bytes are used to represent a character, allowing character sets for many languages to be defined, making it ideal for use on the Net.

URL (*Uniform Resource Locator*) The string describing the location of an Internet page or file, e.g. **http://www.madesimple.co.uk**. A URL is a type of URI (Universal Resource Identifier), which is used to locate Internet resources.

User agent A program which facilitates communication between a user and a web server. A web browser is a user agent, as is the mini-browser on a mobile phone.

Valid An XML document is *valid* if its contents conform to the rules laid down in a DTD.

Web server The computer which holds web pages and associated material, such as XML code and multimedia files. A *client* computer will request data from the web server using HTTP.

Web service: A web server-based application that provides a service to an end customer. Web services generally use XML messages to communicate with other similar applications on the Internet.

Weblog A type of online journal that uses a dated format for user entries. Also known as a 'blog'.

Well-formed An XML document that adheres to XML grammatical rules. If a document is not well-formed the page is in error and will not be displayed.

WML (*Wireless Markup Language*) The XML variant used to program portable Internet sites for mobile phones. Pages are built from a series of interlinked 'cards' and are optimised to fit in the small memory of portable devices.

XHTML (*eXtensible HTML*) An adapted version of HTML 4.01 that obeys XML rules.

XLink (*XML Linking Language*) Adds extra hyperlinking functionality to XML documents. The XPointer language is used alongside Xlink to fetch parts of linked documents. As yet there is limited support on browsers for both.

XML (*eXtensible Markup Language*) A metalanguage used for describing electronic documents in a standardised way.

XPath The XML Path Language is a technology for working out how to navigate through documents.

XSL (*eXtensible Stylesheet Language*) A system for describing how a document should look. More powerful than CSS, XSL is used to transform plain XML into other formats.

Index